KIDS'
COMEDIC
MONOLOGUES
THAT ARE
ACTUALLY
FUNNY

KIDS' COMEDIC MONOLOGUES THAT ARE ACTUALLY FUNNY

Edited by

ALISHA GADDIS

APPLAUSE
THEATRE & CINEMA BOOKS
An Imprint of Hal Leonard Corporation

Published in 2016 by Applause Theatre & Cinema Books
An Imprint of Hal Leonard Corporation
7777 West Bluemound Road
Milwaukee, WI 53213

Trade Book Division Editorial Offices
33 Plymouth St., Montclair, NJ 07042

Printed in the United States of America

Book design by UB Communications

Library of Congress Cataloging-in-Publication Data

Names: Gaddis, Alisha, editor.
Title: Kids' comedic monologues that are actually funny / edited by Alisha Gaddis.
Description: Milwaukee, WI : Applause Theatre & Cinema Books, 2016.
Identifiers: LCCN 2016004285 | ISBN 9781495011764 (pbk.)
Subjects: LCSH: Monologues—Juvenile literature. | Acting—Auditions—Juvenile literature. | Comedy sketches—Juvenile literature.
Classification: LCC PN2080 .K45 2016 | DDC 812/.0450817—dc23
LC record available at http://lccn.loc.gov/2016004285

www.applausebooks.com

Contents

Contents   vii

Introduction

FOR KIDS ONLY

You guys! This is so exciting! Isn't acting so incredibly fun?!? You get to pretend to be different people, in different times, in different worlds. Sometimes, you even get paid for it! Playing make believe is so fantastical and whimsically delightful. And making people laugh is even better! The book you are currently holding is a key to unlock even more imagination and wonderment! People who are funny for a living wrote this just for you! Have fun, play, and make people laugh!

FOR THE BIG PEOPLE WHO BELONG TO THE KIDS ONLY

You deserve a big pat on the back! You are helping your little nugget bloom and grow! This book is perfectly appropriate for kids ages five to thirteen, whether they are just shedding their shy skin or are ready to shine in the spotlight. In fact, it was *made* for them—whilst still being hilarious, witty, and smart. Just like YOU GUYS! Next stop—the Oscars!

Alisha Gaddis

God Only Knows

Alisha Gaddis

CHARLIE, 5 to 7

CHARLIE *shares a room with his older brother, Brendan. They are down for the night and* CHARLIE *is trying to have a last-minute nighttime talk.*

CHARLIE   *Pssssttt . . .*

Brendan? Are you asleep?

[*Beat.*]

You aren't now. Ha. Okay. Me neither. What are you doing?

[*Beat.*]

Trying to sleep? Me too.

Mom and Dad are still up. I can hear that crime show on. Brendan . . . can I ask you something?

[*Beat.*]

I just did? Oh. Yeah. Can I ask you something else?

[*Beat.*]

I just did again?

[*Beat.*]

Okay.
Brendan, do you believe in God? Like, really believe?

[*Beat.*]

You do? Me too. But I just don't know how tall God is or where he lives. He has to be taller than Kobe Bryant and a giraffe and that really big tree by my school—because he is in charge of all that stuff. And if heaven is in the clouds and hell is in the center of the Earth, why don't we just fly higher in planes and stop digging new basements? What if we are digging a basement and hell and fire come out! I think that happens in Florida . . . maybe we shouldn't visit Grandma there this year . . .

Do you think God is listening to us right now? How can he listen to everyone at once?

Maybe he has superpowers! He can be invincible and can see through walls and can fly!

Wow.

I want to meet him, but just not right now.

[*Beat.*]

Are you asleep? Brendan . . .

[*No response.*]

God—if you are listening right now, I believe in you. Please watch over us all and especially Brendan, and please can we win the game tomorrow and can someday I fly with you?

Thank you.

Amen.

But Why?

Carla Cackowski

CHARLIE, 5 to 6 (gender neutral)

CHARLIE *is waiting for his/her mom to get off the phone so they can go to the playground.*

CHARLIE   Mom, I'm ready to go to the playground now . . . but why? Okay, fine.

[CHARLIE *shouts into the phone.*]

Hi, Aunt Julie!

Okay Mom, get off the phone . . . But why?

[CHARLIE *bounces up and down.*]

Pleeeeease.

Shoes? But why? I don't need—

Fine!

[CHARLIE *puts on shoes.*]

Okay, I'm ready! Let's go now.

I already said, "Hi." . . . But why? Okay, fine.

[CHARLIE *shouts into the phone.*]

Goodbye, Aunt Julie!

Mom, let's go.

I don't need a jacket . . . but why? I'm not cold . . . but why? I won't get cold. I won't . . . No, I won't.

Mom, get off the phone.

[CHARLIE *bounces around, shouting.*]

Mom, get off the phone, Mom, get off the phone, Mom, why are you on the phone, Mom, you talk too much, Mom—

No, you're being difficult! Me? Nope! . . . But why?! But why?! But why?!

I promise to stop asking it if you get off the phone!

Thank you. Let's go now.

Jacket? But whyyyyyyyyyyyyy?

Stowaway

Leah Mann

OLLIE TUMBLETOWN, 6 to 10

A dirty-looking boy hides in a barrel. He looks up in dismay as a pirate glares down at him. The kid climbs out of the barrel, his face setting into defiance.

OLLIE TUMBLETOWN Took long enough to find me, ya scurvy scallywag. I been hidin' in this barrel feasting on your rotten apples for days. I hope your piratin' is better 'n your security.

[*Beat.*]

I knows why you lookin' at me like that, but I won't be apologizing for this. A pirate don't apologize for nothing, and I aim to be a better pirate than any of you limpin' sea dogs. You WANT me on your ship. Jus' wait an' see. I'm all sorts of helpful and fierce as a kraken. Not that I've ever seen a kraken but I read the stories and I'm tellin' ya, I got all the fight and ferocity in me as any sea monster plus wiles to boot.

[*Beat.*]

You think I'm full of cow pies from toes to top, don'tchya? I know that look. I got a ma and da, like any man. I isn't full of hot air—I full of trouble and hard work and all sorts of cleverness. I'll start swabbing an' scrubbing and pealin' potatoes, I isn't proud. I is ambitious and mean to captain me own ship one day, and that's why you're gonna put me ta work instead of tossing me overboard.

[*Beat.*]

I isn't a child . . . Maybe in years but not in fury.

I know work—hard work—and if I'm gonna sleep like the dead, weary and hurtin' from my day, let it be on the wide open sea. I lurv it more than me ma and da, who fed me and clothed me so's I could plow the fields and muck the stables and never see nothin' of the world.

[*Beat.*]

Will I miss me old man? Ay, he told a right good tale and taught me many a dirty song. I'll miss me brothers and sisters too, but half of 'em will fall to sickness and makin' babies anyways. And me ma? Me precious ma who gave me life? I won't miss her a moment. Already forgot her face. Couldn't tell you whether those hard eyes are blue or brown or how many fingers she's got on the hand she uses to smack us with a spoon or waggle at me da for talkin' dirty in front of us.

[*Beat.*]

Was her behavin' like a mad heathen brought on by my da's straying eyes or my own sass mouth and troubling makin'? Can't say. Don't matter, if ya ask me, a mother is made to love her eldest no matter how many times he cuts his sisters' hair in the night or sings sea shanties at the top of his lungs when the babes are sleepin'.

[*Beat.*]

Do you know any sea shanties? I'd think you do, bein' a pirate and all; but I don't make assumptions, seein' as I was born a hundred miles from the sea even though I've the salt of the ocean flowin' through me veins. I write me own shanties too—'tis me special talent.

[*Singing loudly.*]

OOOHH . . . A sailor loves the water
More than he loves his mother
A sailor loves the sea
More than he loves biscuits and tea
Me mum's real mean and tillin's a bore
I'd rather be a man with an oar—

[*Beat.*]

You don't look impressed.

[*Beat.*]

I got ones that aren't about me ma!

[Beat.]

Don't be pointin' at the plank. I isn't going to walk it. You'll have to drag me down it and I'll take ya wid me.

[Beat.]

If I promise not to sing, can I be a cabin boy?

[Beat.]

Kitchen boy?

[Beat.]

Privy boy?

[Beat.]

Tell me mum?! Ya wouldn't. Ya couldn't. We's too far out ta sea! Winds are no good! She can't read! Pigeons don't go to me house! Iffin ya tell me mum, I'll run off that plank and jump right inta a shark's gullet! Ya want that on your conscience?

[Beat.]

Damned pirates ain't got no morals!

A Pony for Christmas

Dana Weddle

ANNA, 10 to 12

The setting is the living room in ANNA's *house, Christmas morning.*

ANNA [*Clearly disappointed.*] So these are all the presents, huh? Looks like there aren't any more under the tree. All clear? Huh. What do you know. That's all the presents! [*Beat.*] Did everybody get what they wanted? I sure hope so. Everybody deserves to be their happiest on Christmas morning. [*Nods head.*] Yep. Christmas morning, when dreams come true! Wow! [*Claps hands together.*] Look at all these *three* things I got. Gosh. It's so funny. I didn't even ask for these cowboy boots. Man. Cowboy boots. What a surprise to get this gift I didn't even ask for . . . but totally love! And check out these Wranglers! Wrangler jeans. I didn't even know what Wrangler jeans were until today. I am learning so much on Christmas morning! [*Getting emotional.*] Wow, have you ever seen a more gorgeous pair of Wrangler jeans? A perfect, totally random pair of Wrangler cowboy jeans to go with these totally *not-requested* cowboy boots that I didn't even know I could love SO MUCH because I didn't even ask for them! And this cowgirl shirt, wow! Just wow! [*Sniffling.*] Wow is all I have to say when gazing upon such beauty! [*Losing it.*] I will be the only one at school ever in the history of time to wear these clothes in public. [*Crying at this point.*] And NO ONE will make fun of me. Ever! Wow! Lucky me!

What did I ask for? Dad, come on, everyone knows what I asked for. [*Wiping away the tears.*] Christmas isn't about gifts anyway, right? It's about togetherness and building snowmen and hot apple cider and—

I mean, I asked for a PONY, a real-life pony. EVERYONE HEARD ME ASK FOR A PONY! Right??!

What a silly thing to ask for. A pony! I mean, all those riding lessons were just for fun anyway. Just a hobby, really. No one ever gets a pony for Christmas. So silly . . . a pony . . . [*Wistful.*] . . . that you can ride . . . and brush . . . and braid its mane and take to shows and win blue ribbons and love and cherish. A real-life dream-come-true pony . . . [*Then.*] that nobody ever gets as a gift, ever! Oh, that's so silly. [*Laughs.*] Real gifts are the unexpected—the boots, the Wrangler jeans . . . the . . . [*Feigning excitement, fighting back the tears.*] *COWBOY CLOTHES!!!*

[*Beat.*]

Huh? [*Confused.*] To the window? [*She steps forward, peering through the window.*] Why do you want me to look out the window? [*Beat.*] Umm . . . Dad . . . [*Stunned.*] There's a horse in the driveway. Did you know there was a—Whose horse? *It's mine?!* My horse? You got me a—*a pony? YOU GOT ME A PONY FOR CHRISTMAS?!!*

[*Beat.* ANNA *is stunned; we see the realization that she has gotten a real horse wash over her face.*]

[*Bursts into tears.*] You are so mean!!!!!!!

Look Look Look But But Butts

Alessandra Rizzotti

SEAN, 7

SEAN *is on the playground with his friends. He is hyperactive, or has ADHD. He's definitely misunderstood and doesn't necessarily have social cues.*

SEAN   Do you have a Transformer? I have a Transformer. Do you have a Ninja Turtle? I have a Ninja Turtle. Look look look. Look at that over there! It's a plane in the sky!

[*He points to the sky and starts running in circles.*]

Hah-ha!!!! This is FUNNNNNNNN!

[*He starts to somersault and do cartwheels.*]

Hey, Tommy, come here and show me a trick. Any trick! I don't care what it is. Just do a trick! Can you fly, jump, roll your tummy, or stand on your toes? Can you do it all? I can! I can!

[*He starts to roll his tummy, then stands on his toes, then points to his butt.*]

Look look look. But But Butt! See?????? Llalalalalallala. I am a superhero! Are you a superhero? I have a little thing called feelings! They're my superpower. When I express them, people are like, WOAH, and then they don't mess with me!

[*He starts fistfighting the air, then runs in circles again.*]

Catch me if you can! Tommy, Tommy, Tommy, catch me!

[*Tommy catches* SEAN. SEAN *laughs and gets out of breath.*]

Ha-ha-ha-ha!!!!! This is fun! Are you ready for our math test? I feel like I'm not ready yet because I don't know how to add all the numbers in the world and I get anxious and sometimes I scramble all the numbers and then I don't know how to add at all! Do you know how to add all the numbers in the world? But but butt. [*He points to his butt.*] I can't!

Well sure, we can't know everything! But we can know some things and I know that I have a hard time with math and reading and even being a person, sometimes! I can't remember everything. Can you? My mom says that that's okay. That some people are more special than others and my specialness is having strong feelings, which means I cry more than some people sometimes, but that's okay! I'm allowed! And you're allowed!

Look look look! But But Butttt! [*He points to his butt, then the sky.*] There's a blue bird! Do you see it in the distance? Let's run to the trampoline! I'll race you and then let's eat all the gumdrops we can find in the universe!

[*He runs off, holding his butt.*]

Babysitters Shouldn't Have to Order Pizza

Gina Nicewonger

DELANEY, 6 to 9 (gender neutral)

DELANEY *is speaking to Samantha, the babysitter, in the kitchen.*

DELANEY   Samantha, I bet most of the kids you babysit just want you to order a pizza, but babysitters shouldn't have to order pizza, and I'm not like most kids. I *love* eating a big healthy salad. Strong bodies, strong minds—that's what Mom always says.

Sure, I can show you where everything is, Samantha. There's spinach and carrots in the fridge drawer. We should slice up that big tomato. Can you believe tomatoes are rich in nutrients and taste better than candy? I *love* eating a big healthy salad!

Oooh, let's chop up some mushrooms and add some of that shredded mozzarella on top? Did you know that low-fat mozzarella provides both calcium *and* vitamin D? Boy, I *love* eating a big healthy salad!

You know what Mom always puts on top? Multigrain croutons! To add a healthy crunch. Problem is that we're out of baked croutons. There is some dough in the back of the fridge. It wouldn't take too long to spread it out and stick it in the oven. In fact, we could just sprinkle the chopped tomatoes over the dough, and put the big healthy salad on top. Well, maybe just the mushrooms and mozzarella. I don't know how spinach and carrots would do in the oven. In fact, I'm pretty sure Dad has a secret stash of pepperonis behind the butter. I think pepperonis would be pretty good with our salad, and I won't tell if you won't.

No Samantha, I've never actually tried this exact salad. But, if it doesn't turn out, we could always order a pizza.

Love Potion

Leah Mann

SEVERIN THE APPRENTICE, 10 to 12

SEVERIN THE APPRENTICE *looks around the Master Wizard's Tower with greed.*

SEVERIN THE APPRENTICE   Finally, I'm alone! Wizard Mervin is all talk talk talk talk talk . . . Putter putter putter . . .

I thought he'd never leave, but if I know Wizard Mervin—and I do because I spend an average of twenty-one hours of the day with him—he'll be at the university getting drunk with his old buddies while they turn each other's beards into spaghetti until three a.m.

So let's get started. Carefully, of course. "Haste makes waste," as Merv always says. Heavens, I wish I was allowed to call him Merv. Curvy Mervy . . . he'd abhor that—but he can't keep eating six meals a day and buttering his apples like he does if he wants to keep a slim figure.

Milk thistle, toad sweat, sparrow tears, ground harpy gallstone, powdered narwhal horn, toenail of toddler, plaque scraped from the tooth of a ogre . . . check, check, check . . . check across the board.

One eyelash, one hair, and one scab picked from the knee of my beloved—the beauteous, the bountiful, the brilliant, the sharp-witted and clear-eyed Margaretta. No simple task, as girls like Margaretta don't go strewing their eyelashes about.

[*Sighs.*]

Ahhh, Margaretta. For Margaretta I would travel through the six lands and over the twelve oceans on a raft built from nothing but twigs and dreams to slay a dragon. I'd slave at her feet from now until eternity for a chance at a kind word. I'd rot in the dankest cell of the darkest dungeon for one of her smiles cast my way.

[*Beat.*]

If this doesn't go well, I will be tossed in the dungeon.

[*Beat.*]

Creating and administering a *love* potion is not allowed for so many reasons, and no apprentice is permitted to create any potions . . . If this were to backfire, then I'd be wrapped in irons in a cell not merely dark and dank but undoubtedly riddled with rodents, mold, and feces.

Surely they wouldn't torture a promising young boy only ten and two years of age for such an understandable crime? My angelic, youthful face should ensure a mere "boys will be boys" slap on the wrist.

[*Beat.*]

. . . Of course love potions are forbidden to *everyone*, not just apprentices.

"The human heart may not be tampered with. To toy with the very spirit of another being is the darkest form of black magic and the most immoral sin in all of wizardry."

But that has to be an exaggeration! It's just a potion. I simply slip it into her morning concoction of blended bananas and mammoth milk, and later that day when her eyes happen upon me during evening meal in the castle, she realizes that despite the differences in age, height, and social status that I am handsome, clever, and would make a most satisfactory companion.

It is only a matter of time before I have a growth spurt, and in several years—seven or so—I'll be the same age as her.

[*He plucks out an eyelash and a hair, searches his body for a scab.*]

How do I not have any scabs on me!? I only recently recovered from the pox.

[*Beat.*]

I suppose I could prick myself and hope my blood congeals quickly.

[*Beat.*]

I'm not very fond of blood though.

[*Beat.*]

Especially when it's mine.

[*He thinks hard and deep.*]

Is it possible that this is a BAD idea?

[*Beat.*]

Truly, if Margaretta is the one for me, she will see that without artificial means. She is no prize to be won, no empty-headed object to be tricked into liking me . . .

There is no need for me to shed by blood, to risk punishment—to risk my very life! Not that she isn't worth the risk—I would indeed rot in prison for a smile from her, but that smile should be given freely.

[*He scratches at his head in intense deliberation.*]

Huh. Interesting development. That feels like a most satisfactory scab.

[*Beat.*]

Now this is a dilemma. One for the philosophy books! My insides are all astir with confusion. Do I complete the spell, eliminate Margaretta's free will, and risk my life all for love? Or do I just . . . I don't know? Take up jousting?

[*Beat.*]

No!

[*Beat.*]

I shan't start jousting in place of pursuing my love.

[*Beat.*]

Much too much blood. Mayhap the chess club . . .

Skipping Kindergarten

Kayla Cagan

RONNIE, 5 (gender neutral)

The setting is the family's living room. RONNIE (short for either Veronica or Ronald) addresses her/his mom and dad about why she/he shouldn't attend kindergarten.

RONNIE   Mommy. Dad. I'm really glad you could make it to our family meeting tonight. I have something we need to discuss—something I think you should consider very carefully. Are you ready?

[*Pause.*]

I'm going to have to skip kindergarten this year.

I know what you're thinking. Mommy, you were excited to walk me to school for the first day. Dad, you thought I would be a class leader. Those things can both still happen in first grade . . . next year. There's really no reason for me to leave home quite yet, and right now I think I could use a little more "me" time.

Look, I already know my ABCs. I can recite the alphabet forward and backward. Numbers are a cinch. A little confusing in the thousands, but I can figure it out. I can work on my napping and playtime and snacks here at home, and it gives me more time to bond with our new dog, Mr. Lickers, too. I have to make sure he knows he can count on me for walks. It would be awful if he went number one or number two in the house. I know you don't want that to happen. Do you?

And then there's another thing. I am going to have to seriously work on my coloring inside of the lines this year because, as we all know, I'm having difficulty in that particular area. And you don't want me to go to school coloring like a four-year-old, do you? Of course not.

I can tell by the look on your faces that you are surprised by my decision. Of course you are. But trust me, I'm making the right choice here! I'm not ready to go to school yet and you're not ready to let me go to school, right? It makes so much sense. Going too early, too soon, could only lead to disaster . . . huge disasters! We're talking absolutely HUGE, people! Bigger than we could possibly imagine! [RONNIE *makes a funny, crazy explosion sound.*]

[*Pause. Catches breath.*]

So, I'll give you time to consider my decision while I walk Mr. Lickers to the corner. I'm sure, once you discuss it with each other, you will both agree to let me stay home for at least a few more years. It's a win-win situation for all of us.

Formerly Known as E

Emily Brauer Rogers

ELISE, 7

ELISE *speaks to her older sister, Amy, in their playroom that's set up as a school.*

ELISE   [*Whining.*]

I don't want to play school anymore. It's boring since it's always the same. You're the teacher, and I'm the student. What do I want to play? Hmmm.

[*She looks around.*]

I want to play letters. No, not the ABCs. We are the letters.

[*She becomes her character, the letter* E.]

See, I have this problem. You can't see. Look!

[*Holds hands out in the shape of an* F.]

What do I look like? That's right. The letter *F*. But I'm not *F*. I'm *E*! Well, I know. How are you supposed to believe me when I look like *F*'s twin sister? But it's true. It's really me, *E*. Can you see where I used to be *E*? Down here at the bottom.

And I need your help. I have to get my bottom back. I know, I know, it's totally embarrassing, but it's not my fault. It's that evil *O*'s fault. You don't know *O*. I'll tell you, she's been rolling around doing whatever she wants, knocking letters down left and right. She knocked poor *N* over and he looked like *Z* for a few days until *M* and *P* could stand him back up again. Who does she think she is? Everyone in the alphabet has been mad at her for days!

Because she had been earning such a bad reputation, she decided to come steal my bottom and is using it to disguise herself as *Q*. Yeah, that's her. Right over there! With my bottom half. It looks horrible on her—she can't pull it off.

Where's the real *Q*? I don't know, but I know that—here, I'll prove it to you. *Q* . . . oh *Q*? I mean, *O*? See? She didn't look when I said "*Q*," but as soon as I said "*O*," she turned this way. You didn't see it! She ran off. Anytime I get near her, she scatters away to the end of the alphabet. That's why I need your help. If you could just sneak up on her and grab the bottom, I think I could repair it so I'd look like my normal self again.

I know it seems odd, but think about? What is the alphabet without *E*? All those kids singing:

[E *sings, sung to the tune of the "Alphabet Song."*]

A, B, C, D, F, F, G . . .

[E *stops singing, and speaks.*]

It's ridiculous. The end of *E*s everywhere. "Read" will become "rad" and "elephant" will become "lphant." Your "eye" will just be "y." So, that's why you have to help me, *A*. Think if somebody stole your middle. You'd just be an upside down *V*. And what can you do with an upside down *V*, anyway? Please. Please, please, please, please, please, please.

Yes, Yes? You'll help me? Hooray.

[E *does a happy dance.*]

Okay, let's go over here. I have a plan. It includes distraction, a lasso, and pretending that you're a moose.

[E *exits.*]

Hello Klippy!

Josh Hyman

JORDAN, 9 (gender neutral)

It's a winter afternoon during a holiday break from school. A bunch of witty 4th graders were just having a play date at JORDAN's *apartment. But when* JORDAN's *younger sister accidentally destroys a favorite toy, the group is not happy and goes too far with their revenge. After a long "time out,"* JORDAN *tries to plead a case for release, but none of* JORDAN's *arguments or tactics seems to be working. The bedroom is big, with plush stuffed animals on the bed, video games under the TV, all kinds of toys and plenty of books, but* JORDAN *just can't stomach being in there any longer.*

JORDAN   [*Angrily.*] Mom!!!!

[*A beat, then teary-eyed.*]

Mom, I'm sorry! I don't want to be punished anymore. I've already been in my room for two hours! Come on. It's been a tough stretch of solitary confinement in here. I'm sorry!!!

[*A beat, then practical.*]

Look, I know the door isn't locked, Warden. I could have made a run for it, but ya see how good I'm being by asking for parole first? Can I come out now please?

[*A beat, then using the facts to justify the group's actions.*]

We were just teaching the kid a lesson, okay? Look—for the last time, I didn't mean to clip off ALL of Melissa's bangs. I'm sorry. I mean, yes, she's my sister and only five years old, but she's a pain in the neck and she never leaves me alone when my friends are over. It was well deserved. She took my Hello Kitty doll and then pulled the ears off! Like, come on! You cannot . . . ahem, you DO NOT rip the ears off a Hello Kitty doll! No ears, no kitty. Then it's just a Hello Weird-Looking-Lady-With-A-Whiskers-Mustache doll. Who does that? I'm sorry, but she's a little tyrant with a bit of a destruct-o quality. There are rules, Mom. When you screw up, you need to be taught a lesson. Trust me, I let her off easy. The other members in the Hello Kitty Club of 14th Street wanted to shave her eyebrows; I suggested only trimming her bangs. Don't you see, I'm always looking out for her?

[*A beat, seeing the other side.*]

I mean, I suppose you could be right too. I'm not a parent. I don't have a lot of experience with discipline; despite the eighty-seven times I've gotten in trouble since my last birthday (YES! I've been keeping a chart, and NO! I'm not proud that I'm already over seventy-five violations and it's only June).

[*Pause, then digging in.*]

But I think it's also because your instructions don't make sense sometimes. Like if I get a B on a spelling test, you tell me that I should be more like my friends who get As. But then when I give Melissa a little punk-rocker, glam-girl shape-up, because Lisa did it to her sister when she ripped her sticker book, you get all, "I don't care what you're friends are doing!" It's confusing. Pick a life lesson and stick with it, woman! I mean, Mom.

[*A beat, self-punishment.*]

Okay, I'm just going to assume you're getting all this. The door isn't so thick, and I can hear you giggle-breathing out there so I'm guessing this set isn't totally bombing? Look, let's do this. I'll take one for the team. I'll trim my bangs too. Okay? Right up to the hairline. Sister Missy and I will be the sibling weirdos of the building, and if anyone asks, you can just tell them Grandma did it. It's fine, she's losing it anyway and I wouldn't put it past her at this point. Okay? Then, we'll all go downtown and get Mike Tyson face tattoos. JUST KIDDING!

[*A beat, then flattery, begging, and reality all settle in.*]

Mom? Mother . . . ? Fair and Merciful Queen of the Citadel? We cool? You need to let me out now, please! I've confessed and apologized and fallen on my sword.

Seriously, Mom, come on. I have to pee.

Admissions

Alisha Gaddis

LAWRENCE ROQUEFORT CLARENCE STEPHSON, THE THIRD, 5 to 7

LAWRENCE *is sitting in an admission counselor's office wearing a nicely pressed suit and tie.*

LAWRENCE   Okay. Let's make this fast. I've got some calls to make about some deals. My full name is Lawrence Roquefort Clarence Stephson, the third—I do NOT respond to Larry. I know you have got some questions, and I've got some answers. But let's be honest—I AM the answer.

Your school, Nickelbach Cumberbach McClain's Prestigious Academy for the Gifted and Talented was meant for a kid like me.

I play the cello and Suzuki piano, am a chess master, the captain of my lacrosse team the Sherlocks, have trained extensively at the Cordon Bleu, work in hedge funds during the day—and I am six. But unlike other child prodigies—I don't plan on burning out or becoming an addict. I have a fifteen-year plan, see? That is—I plan on retiring on the sunny shores of the Seychelles at the ripe ole age of twenty-one. You should see my stock portfolio! But for now, I need you as a place where I am being "formally educated" and you need me to make your brochure look good.

Let's call this a deal and I will put you in touch with my secretary.

[*Reaches out hand for handshake.*]

I look forward to starting kindergarten here on Tuesday.

The Cold Shoulder: I'll Stop This Car

Leah Mann

MELANIE, 9 to 12

MELANIE, *an obnoxious kid, stands on the side of the road yelling after a minivan that's driving down the road farther and farther away from her.*

MELANIE   Mom! MOOOOOMMMMM!!!

[*Beat.*]

She did it. She actually did it. I can't believe it. This is child abuse. This is insanity!

[*Beat.*]

I'm pretty sure this is illegal. Gosh, this might be history—I should call the news.

My mom could be the first parent in the history of the world to actually stop the car and make her kid walk.

[*Beat.*]

I don't know how far away this is from home, but it seems really far.

Man, and she confiscated my phone for texting while she was trying to "have a talk" with me. Like, you can't text and talk at the same time? I mean, maybe she can't because she's old, but my generation is totally fine multitasking.

[*Beat.*]

I don't think she's coming back. I've never seen her that angry. Mom doesn't usually get angry. She's cool as a cucumber, chillin' like Bob Dylan, calm like the last five minutes of yoga class.

I guess I should be walking home. I hope I can find it, since I don't carry around a map of the town in my back pocket in case my own MOTHER decides to strand me by the side of the road. Next time I leave the house I'll bring an atlas with me just in case.

I shouldn't have yelled at her to stop butting into my personal life with all of her questions. Grabbing the steering wheel probably didn't help either, or spilling hot tea all over her lap . . .

Still, it's not cool to abandon me. Parents have to take care of kids, no matter what. That's the rule. It's not my fault I overreact sometimes. I wish I could be Zen like Mom, but I'm not. I'm like Dad but without any anti-anxiety medication.

What . . . if . . . I *don't* walk home?

That'd be a twist.

What if I turned around and headed back into town? What if I walked all the way back past tutoring and went to the bus station and bought a ticket to Grandma's house? I have enough money. It'll take three hours to get there. Mom would wait a while and then feel bad—I HOPE—and come back looking for me.

But I'll be gone, so she'll start driving around and she can't track me on GPS because she has my phone and then she'll have an anxiety attack and know what it's like!

Ha! Maybe then she won't get mad the next time I lose it.

Meanwhile, I'll be sitting pretty at Grandma's eating those chocolate graham cracker cookies she buys and showing off my new magic tricks. Grandma is a total sucker for my magic tricks. By the time I get there and Grandma calls, my mom will have learned her lesson. She'll be so scared . . .

[*Beat.*]

Being scared is the worst.

Not that I'm a scaredy-cat.

Not generally. I'm maybe a little scared right now.

I should have done my counting exercise to calm down instead of kicking the back of the seat and throwing her purse out the window.

Her purse! I should find it. Then she'll forgive me.

[*Beat.*]

Plus there are usually snacks in it. And tissues, which I might need because it's chilly out and not because I'm crying.

[*Looking around, squinting, trying to spot the purse.*]

Is that a car?

It's a car! It's a blue car with a bike rack on top and that means . . .

[MELANIE's *head turns as the car drives by without slowing.*]

That someone else has the exact same car as we do.

Home or bus station? Home or bus station? Humiliation or revenge? Grandma and cookies or Mom and apologies? Revenge and cookies SOUNDS better than humiliation and saying I'm sorry.

[*Sighs.*]

I guess it's Grandma's house.

[*Sadly.*]

Oh well, sorry Mom. I wish it didn't have to be this way, but the pluses and minuses speak for themselves.

[*Sees something in the distance.*]

What's that?

[*Beat.*]

Just another blue car with a bike rack.

[*Beat.*]

Mom! MOOOOMMM!!!!

[*Beat.*]

Thank goodness! Who needs chocolate-covered graham crackers? She just buys them at the store.

Now where did I throw that purse?

Family Dog

Keisha Cosand

ADDISON, 11 (gender neutral)

ADDISON, *an older brother or sister, is playing with the "family dog" out in the backyard.*

ADDISON   Come here, boy! Come here! That's a good boy. Sit. Stay.

[ADDISON *pretends to throw an imaginary bone.*]

Yes! Go get it!

[*Imaginary "dog" brings it back.*]

Good boy! Wanna do it again? Let go. You have to let go!

[ADDISON *plays tug-o-war, trying to get pretend bone away from the "dog."*]

I don't want to play tug-o-war. This is fetch! Drop it! If you keep growling, I'm not going to play.

[*"Dog" lets go and* ADDISON *stumbles back a bit.*]

Good boy! Here! [ADDISON *waves the imaginary bone in the "dog's" face.*]

Go get it! [ADDISON *pretends to throw imaginary bone really far across the yard.*]

What?!

[ADDISON *yells back toward the house, responding to his mom's call.*]

We're just playing! Okay! Fine!

[*Still yelling back toward the house at his mom.*]

Yes, I'll stop treating him like a dog! It's your fault! If you would let me have a real dog, I wouldn't have to resort to this! He's fine! He likes it! Look at him! No, I have no idea what therapy costs!

[*To the "dog."*]

Come on, Bobby, get up. Mom says we can't play "dog" any more. I know, YOU ARE good at it. Good little brother.

[ADDISON *speaks condescendingly and pats little brother on the head.*]

Pick up your bone. Good. Now, heel!

[ADDISON *pats his/her left leg to get the little brother in line, and walks off stage.*]

Hippie Town

Cooper McHatton

MONICA, 10

MONICA *has just moved away from the city to a little country town nearby with her family. She sits in front of a computer talking to a friend of hers in the city on video chat, telling her about life in her new town.*

MONICA   My Mom always said WE were the "hippies" of the family. I think it's because we like to eat organic foods and we love trees. I guess that's why my parents thought it was a good idea to move to our new home in this little town. But now that we're here, I don't think we're hippies.

I've met some.

I mean first there's our neighbors. The guy in the house next to us sells kale at the farmer's market and has this long dreadlocked hair. But that's not the weird part—he walks around only wearing a TOGA!

[*Beat.*]

A toga. It's like those clothes the ancient Greeks and Romans wore. And he has a purple butterfly painted on his face.

[*Beat.*]

Yes I'm serious!

[*Beat.*]

And then there's this other lady that roller-skates in front of our house every morning completely naked except for little starfish things like a mermaid.

[*Beat.*]

It only gets weirder.

[*Beat.*]

No, it's true. At lunchtime every day at school, there are kids just eating seaweed!

[*Beat.*]

Then I got invited to a birthday party and there wasn't any cake!

[*Beat.*]

No! No desserts at all. They said it's because their moms don't allow them to eat sugar or flour or . . .

[*Beat.*]

Yes. Really.

[*Beat.*]

Oh my God! And the presents! Not one present came from a store! And this one family even got this little kid a skinned rabbit that they killed themselves!

[*Beat.*]

Yes. An actual rabbit skin. Like a dead bunny.

[*Beat.*]

I totally swear I am not making this up. This is how it is here. One day I got an ice-cream cone and dropped it outside the store and these two kids attacked it and were eating off the ground!

[*Beat.*]

No I'm not lying. Like, they were actually licking it off the sidewalk. It was gross.

[*Beat.*]

I try and tell my new friends about my old life and they act like I'm from Mars, and I'm like, dudes, it's like an hour from here, and they just stare at me.

[*Beat.*]

No, they never leave here. Like ever. They sit in drum circles at the park and talk about how the government is poisoning us while their little kids are bathing in the fountain.

[*Beat.*]

Yeah, I really miss you too. I mean I kinda like it here. The air smells like flowers, well except when the wind changes. This lady down the street poops in her yard. She doesn't believe in plumbing.

I Am Not a Princess

Marisol Medina

TARYN, 7

TARYN, *a tomboy, is playing in a sandbox outside her home when she gets a surprise visit from her girlie-girl friend* MATTIE, *who is looking for some answers.* TARYN *tries to give them as gently as she can.*

TARYN   Oh hi, Mattie.

It's true. I'm not going to your princess birthday party. [*Quickly changes the topic.*] We can get some frozen yogurt, though! Like the movie? *Frozen?* Your favorite? [*Sings.*] *Let it go! Let it go!* [*Nervously laughs. Stops. Joke failure.*]

It's not like you really need me for your birthday. You have Loretta, Madison, and Ashley going in pink, blue, and purple princess gowns. And then there's you in that . . . [*Looks for the right word.*] really big off-orange princess costume with scrunchy silver wings and unicorn hair in a tight glitter-sprayed bun. Who can compete with that?

No, Mattie. I don't need your green princess costume from last year. Or the magenta one. Or the teal-colored one. It's okay, I don't care if the magic wand really zaps people—I just don't want to be a princess!!

[TARYN *gasps. She can't believe she said it out loud.*]

I don't. Why should any girl want to? Real princesses have to starve themselves and pretend to like horse races. They don't go to balls and wear fun, poufy dresses all the time like you do; they go to "events" and wear old queen dress suits that are knee length and no fun. And the fantasy version's even worse! After getting kidnapped and almost killed, your prize is a stupid Prince Charming?! Sure he's cute and slays dragons, but aside from a castle and some babies for the kingdom, what else can he give you? "They lived happily ever after?" You know what that means? Translation: "The rest of their lives turned out so boring, no one wanted to write about it." I don't want boring, Mattie. I want to be a woman. I want adventure. I want to be an archaeologist. I want to be Indiana Jones.

Yes, Indiana Jones. The old guy from the Disneyland ride and four really good old movies?!

[*Defiant.*] That's not weird—it's smart.

[*Now getting extra huffy.*] Well, while you're sitting around wasting your time on learning how to put on too much makeup for an eight-year-old, I'll be learning how to find lost historical treasures AND how to escape Nazis.

[*The words now tumble out faster and faster.*] I'll know how to fight for myself and ride horses and drive motorcycles and army trucks and airplanes and submarines and Goodyear balloons and shoot guns and whip whips and eat monkey brains so I don't look like a bad guest.

Girls don't need to be pretty and taken care of. They should want to be intelligent and travel the world and be a professor in a school and have creepy girls say they love them on their eyelids and be so popular they have to crawl out of their office window just to get a bite to eat!

That's who I want to dress up like! That's the dress-up birthday party I'll go to whenever you, Loretta, Madison, or Ashley are finally girl enough to have one! And when you do have that birthday party, my color for my costume will be beige and brown!

You'll have to find your own.

I'll Never

Alessandra Rizzotti

LYDIA, 12

LYDIA *just found out her social studies grade. She's more than panicked. She talks to her best friend after school as they wait for their parents to pick them up.*

LYDIA It's really the end of the world, Stacy. I got a B+ on my social studies test. Now I'll never get on honor roll and I'll never go to college. I'll never get married and I'll never be a CEO. I mean, this is real, Stacy. I can't handle middle school if it's going to continue like this. I keep thinking about how my mother really never succeeded in life because of her C+ report card, and I'm just teetering on the edge of that, on the brink. I'm potentially getting there, you know? I really thought I understood the Shang Dynasty. Well, here's to knowing NOTHING!

Don't tell me that, Stacy. I can beat myself up as much as I want to. Just because you got a B+ too doesn't mean YOU'RE doomed. You at least have an affluent family and a dog. I live in an apartment with a fish and a single mother. The odds of me succeeding in life are much lower than yours. You'll get into an Ivy League. I'll go to a Cal State. You'll go corporate. I'll probably do a nonprofit or some sort of startup that will never become Google. You'll live in Beverly Hills. I'll find myself in South Los Angeles. That's just how it is, and believe me, I'm not complaining. Just stating facts.

Are you going to basketball practice after school? Because now I think I can't. I have too much to study now about the Xiu Dynasty. I don't want to confuse dynasties again on our next test, even though it's in two weeks. You'll have to tell the coach that I'm not feeling well. He'll get it . . . No, Stacy—it doesn't make sense for me to exercise when my mind can't be on the game. It has to be on China and emperors!

[LYDIA *notices a car pulling up to the curb.*]

Oh, my mom is here. I'll see you tomorrow. Please cover for me. God knows if I don't pass this next test, I'll probably fail life.

[LYDIA *gets up off the bench.*]

Don't say that, Stacy! I can't rely on sports to get me to college. I have to rely on my BRAINS! You know I'm left-handed anyways. Things in sports never work out for us lefties. I'll see you tomorrow, unless I die of a panic attack. Ha!

[*She yells at her mom.*]

Hurry up, Mom! I have to study right now!

Imagine That

Mark Alderson

CHRISTOPHER, 7

CHRISTOPHER *and his best friend are in* CHRISTOPHER*'s bedroom.* CHRISTOPHER *sits at the edge of the bed and begins to talk to his best friend.*

CHRISTOPHER   Hi, Mr. Jinksy. Thank you for seeing me today. Would you like a cookie? My mom made them fresh and I told her to make them a little burnt, just how you like them. Oh, you don't want a cookie? You sure? Because I am only going to offer it once . . .

[CHRISTOPHER *sets down the tray of cookies next to his friend, and wipes his hands.*]

Now, let's get down to what I wanted to talk to you about. As you know, we've been friends for, well, since I could count. You've helped me through thunderstorms, cleaning my room, and even offered me advice on what clothes I should wear, and I can't thank you enough.

[*Sigh.*]

But it needs to stop, Mr. Jinksy.

You see, I know you're real but I also know I imagined you, so I think it's time to say good-bye. It's not that I don't love our time together or that I imagined another friend—not at all. The reason for this parting is because I think you and I both knew this day would come and it's up to me to be the one who breaks the bond.

Listen, this isn't completely good-bye. I wouldn't mind it at all if you dropped by every once in a while on holidays or for big life events—just give me a heads-up so I can make myself available. I'm almost eight and I have a lot coming up.

I hope you didn't think I was just going to cast you off into the dark world, alone. No, I set up some meetings of younger kids in the neighborhood that would love your company; most of them have the same sense of humor as you, so it'll be a great match.

Thank you for everything, Mr. Jinksy. Good luck in life, and I hope to see you again soon.

[CHRISTOPHER *performs an intricate handshake with his imaginary friend and waves good-bye after wiping a tear from his face.*]

Wait, Mr. Jinksy. I changed my mind! I'm not ready to lose a friend. Come back! I was wrong!

[CHRISTOPHER *looks around the room.*]

Mr. Jinksy?

[*Checks another spot.*]

MR. JINKSY?!?

[*Finally, under the bed.*]

Mr. Jinksy!!! Whew! Glad you are still here. Sorry about that. I must have low blood sugar. Wanna cookie?

[CHRISTOPHER *takes a bite from one of the cookies.*]

Blegh! Mom! Can we make some new cookies? Mr. Jinksy says he wants them more burnt!

Don't Worry, Mom. Nothing Happened.

Andy Goldenberg

PHOENIX, 8 to 10 (gender neutral)

PHOENIX *confronts his/her mom in her bedroom during her favorite afternoon TV show.*

PHOENIX   Hey, Mom! Sorry to barge in on your alone time. I know it's the only chance you get to have a minute to yourself and you've told us repeatedly not to disturb you during *The Ellen Show*. I just wanted to tell you how much I love you.

Nothing's wrong. Everything's great. Couldn't be better. I'm the luckiest kid in the world. To have a mother like you taking care of me? Please! You were in labor with me for over thirty hours, remember? Trust me. I'm aware of just how lucky I am. Thank you. From the bottom of my heart. It's an honor to be a part of this family.

I don't want anything. I promise. I already have everything I could ever hope for, the most important being a loving, understanding parent who was once a child herself. Who knows what it means to be young. Who is STILL young. I mean, look at that haircut! I don't know if I mentioned it, but you look amazing. You're the best! Best Mom Ever! How do you do it? Seriously? What's your secret? Magic?

I didn't do anything. I swear. Kind of funny, really. I was just sitting in my room by myself, working on the homework that Mrs. Amendola assigned, and . . . I'm sorry if I freaked you out . . . but this is just something that I've been wanting to tell you for a really long time and couldn't figure out how to work it into any conversation without feeling super lame. But I also didn't want to waste one more minute with you thinking that I took your generosity for granted, and so I thought what better time than right now, right? Unexpected. [*Blows her a kiss.*] *Mwah!*

No, nothing's broken. Is something broken? Did you hear something break? I just really wanted to make sure you knew how much I appreciate your smile and your kindness. There are kids all over the world who don't have a mother half as nice as you. Hell, even Richie's mom won't drive him to school or pack him a lunch or come to his softball game. His dad's not any better. He's barely home. A doctor. Always on call. Like I said, luckiest kid in the world.

Tuesday. It's Tuesday. Just a regular weekday, nothing special. I'm sorry. I didn't mean to freak you out. Just relax. For once! Take a load off. Enjoy your show. I really just wanted to tell you how much you mean to me. Obviously I don't say it enough, but I want to change that. Starting now. Starting today. I love you. So much.

Oh, and I think Josh ran away.

The Thing

Carla Cackowski

ANNE, 12

ANNE *is eating lunch in the cafeteria at school, talking to her four best friends.*

ANNE   So, look, here's the thing . . . well, actually, before I tell you "the thing." you have to promise me you won't tell anyone. Seriously. You are my four best friends, so you each have to swear that you won't tell anyone what I'm about to tell you until I'm ready to tell other people, and then you can tell other people too. Pinky-swear.

[*She pinky-swears each of her four best friends.*]

My parents sat my brother and I down last night after dinner and told us they're getting a divorce.

Yeah. Thanks, but before you give me your condolences or feel really sorry for me or whatever you were going to do, I have to tell you "the thing" . . .

The first thing that popped into my head when they told us they're getting a divorce wasn't "Oh no, that's terrible!" or

"You can't break up our family!" The first thing I thought was "My life is going to be so much more interesting now!"

Is that terrible? Is that like, the most terrible thing you've ever heard? Please don't tell anyone! I'm only saying it to you because you're the four closest people to me on planet Earth and I was sure you wouldn't judge me. You're not, are you?

My parents fight all the time. They can't even sit and watch the same TV show without getting into a fight about it. When they get divorced, I won't have to hear my mother scream that sports "Give her a headache!" or hear my father shout "*True Blood* is unrealistic and pornographic!" When my parents get divorced, I'll be able to finally watch television in peace. Who knows? Maybe when my parents get divorced and have separate televisions in their separate houses, I'll get to pick what we're watching!

When my parents get divorced, I'm going to get to have two bedrooms. So that means that I can pull out all the Taylor Swift posters I hid under my bed because they didn't fit on my walls and put them on my new walls in my second bedroom! I'll also have two Christmases, two birthday parties, two cars to borrow when I turn sixteen, two fridges to eat food from, two closets to fill with clothes!

Finally, when my parents get divorced, I will, of course, actually be very upset, probably even depressed, so just think of all the awesome creativity that will pour out of me while I'm trying to deal with my depression. Some of our favorite artists have divorced parents! Selena Gomez, Emma Watson, Rihanna, Justin Timberlake, Demi Lovato, the OLSEN TWINS! Seriously, it's true—I googled it last night right after my parents told me they're getting a divorce.

Thanks for listening. You really are the dearest, kindest, bestest friends a girl could ever ask for. I feel so much better. Really, truly. So much, in fact, I think I'm ready to tell other people about "the thing." Yes, that means you can tell other people now too . . . Make sure you emphasize how much more interesting my life is going to be when my parents get divorced, okay?

Wedding Bears

Bri LeRose

KATRINA, 10

KATRINA is holding two stuffed bears and talking to an imaginary audience of other toys in her playroom.

KATRINA   Dearly beloved, we are gathered here today to bring together two bears, Christopher McFurry and Miss Fuzzy Face, who used to be called Miss Bear, who used to be called Katrina Jr. These two bears are super in love, and we are all here today to watch them get joined together in holy marriage.

Christopher McFurry and Miss Fuzzy Face met two years ago, on my birthday, because I introduced them to each other. You're welcome. It was love at first site for the bears, and they could talk about anything together. They found out that they both liked tigers, jump roping, and gym class. Clearly, they had a lot in common, and they started being boyfriend and girlfriend right away. Their first date was to the trampoline place, and neither of them got hurt or had to sit down at all.

Miss Fuzzy Face knew she was going to marry Christopher
after that.

She proposed to him because she wanted to. He said yes
because she's smart and beautiful and he'd be crazy not to say
yes. This was two days ago. It has been a very fast engagement,
and they wanted me to say thank you to their friends and
family for making the trip out for their wedding, because they
know it's last-minute and everybody is busy. Especially you,
Papa Bear. They know you had to come all the way from
Texas, and they're so happy you're here.

Love is beautiful. Sometimes, people in love look at each other
like this [KATRINA *makes a silly, dreamy face like she's in love.*]
Sometimes, they hold hands all day no matter where they go.
Sometimes, they just sit around and read the paper and don't
even talk to each other, even though that might seem boring.
If you're in love, nothing is boring as long as you're with your
love person. I know Christopher McFurry and Miss Fuzzy
Face are each other's love persons.

So. Christopher McFurry, do you take this bear to be your
lawfully wedded wife, to have and to hold, as long as you both
shall live? [KATRINA *whispers "I do," like it's coming from
Christopher.*]

And Miss Fuzzy Face, do you take this bear to be your lawfully
wedded husband, to have and to hold, as long as you both shall
live? [KATRINA *whispers "Uh-huh," like it's coming from Miss*

Fuzzy Face.] Then by the power invented in me by myself, I now pronounce you bear and bear. You may kiss the bear.

[KATRINA *makes the bears kiss in a loud, silly way.*]

Okay, that's enough. Don't be gross.

[KATRINA *whispers "Sorry," like it's coming from Christopher.*]

Trouble in History Class

Tiffany E. Babb

STEPHEN/STEPHANIE, 7 to 10 (gender neutral)

STEPHEN/STEPHANIE *is in the living room, speaking to the babysitter.*

STEPHEN/STEPHANIE Today at school we were learning about the Trojan War. Mr. Kinney (that's my teacher) told us that the whole war got started because of a squabble over who had the right to marry this lady. *Helen of Troy.*

[*Beat.*]

So I figure, all right. These things happen. Especially if you're the most beautiful lady in the world. But in the end Helen's gonna be the one to decide who she wants to marry, right?

[*Beat.*]

Wrong. Apparently, she gets stolen from her home. And—*you won't believe this*—then she gets stolen again! Like, what is it with all these people stealing people? That's not what love is supposed to be!

[*Beat.*]

Then again, Mom always says that she stole Momma's heart the moment she laid eyes on her, but I'm pretty sure it stopped there.

[*Beat.*]

Anyways. So Mr. Kinney decides to end class by saying that this whole war got started just because one lady was too pretty, and I was like WOAH. It wasn't her fault that she was pretty— it seemed like it was everyone else's fault for fighting over her and then bringing even more people into the fight. This whole thing could have been avoided if at the very start, someone had just asked Helen who she wanted to marry!

[*Beat.*]

Or if she wanted to marry anyone at all.

[*Beat.*]

And then I got detention for talking back to the teacher. And for standing on a desk during History. And Mom pretended to be angry at me, and Momma told me she was proud of me.

[*Beat.*]

So . . . can I go to the park now?

Gross, Grandma. Gross!

Mike McAleer

PATRICK, 8 to 12

PATRICK *is sitting in his grandparents' living room. He needs to take a break from doing his homework and let off some steam.*

PATRICK   Grandpa, I don't know if you've ever had to deal with any real emotional stuff in your life, but right now I've got something brewing inside of me, and it's hot. I mean like something that has taken over my brain and won't let me concentrate on anything else I'm doing. It's something gross, it's something that needs to be stopped, and it's something that I'm afraid will break up this family unless you can help. It's Grandma's breath, and it smells like dead animals. Not like Chicken McNuggets, but like a dead skunk. I'm sitting in there doing my homework, and she leans over my shoulder and says, "Patrick, your work is outstanding! My grandson. You are so smart!" Nice of her, right? Well, then it happens . . . my nose starts to burn like it's full of lava. *Dead* lava. *Dead* lava with a *dead* skunk spraying *dead* stuff out of its *dead* tail. And I say, "Gross, Grandma. Gross," but she thinks I'm talking about being embarrassed or something. But I'm not—I'm just in pain.

[PATRICK *thinks for a moment.*]

I mean I love Grandma. She always cheers for me at soccer practice and gives me gifts on my birthday and talks to me when I'm feeling down . . . usually not as close to my face, though, thank God. I don't know, maybe it's not *that* bad. Anyway, thank you for listening, Grandpa . . . .

[PATRICK *looks at his grandpa.*]

Are those your teeth in a glass, Grandpa? Gross, Grandpa. Gross!

Freedom Fighter

Leah Mann

JAY, 10 to 14 (gender neutral)

JAY *climbs on top of the teacher's desk and demands the attention of his/her classmates.*

JAY   Classmates. Classmates!

[*Clears his/her throat.*]

CLASSMATES!!

[*Beat.*]

Thank you.

Ahem. Friends, Classmates, New Kid . . . Today is a day like no other. "Why?" you ask. . . . *Shhhh!* Don't actually ask! "Why?" you think quietly in your head. Because today is the day we stand up and say, "Enough!"

Enough with the homework! Enough with the tests! Enough with "quiet down" and "behave"! Enough with reading lists and spelling bees! We are kids only once, and we'll be adults for WAYYY longer. Now is our time to be young, to be free, to have fun and explore.

How many grown-ups diagram sentences for their jobs? Grammar teachers. That's IT. They're the only ones. How many grown-ups do math in their heads or with a pencil and paper? Zero! They use calculators and computers. How many grown-ups know or care about what the world capitals are or what the main export of Zimbabwe is? I don't know, but probably not very many.

You know why we're in school all day? Because they don't want to take care of us so they pay teachers to keep us oppressed while our parents go to their jobs. Well I say NO MORE! It's time for revolution and it starts with a single kid—that's me. Then it spreads to a class—that's you.

Get up out of those plastic chairs and away from those round tables. Throw your folders on the floor, break those pencils, smash those crayons. It's time to get loud, it's time to get proud—we are KIDS and we deserve to be FREE.

"How do we get free?" you may ask . . . in your heads! Jeez, I'm giving a speech here! Don't interrupt.

I have a plan. We rebel. We don't organize, we DISorganize. We make a mess; we kidnap the principal. We tie up the teachers; we stick those gold stars on their faces and test booklets down their throats. We open the windows and play Red Rover even though it's prohibited, and if someone gets hurts we'll untie the school nurse to help them. We have recess all day and when we go home we have our parents sign fake permission slips so we can wander the streets, and if someone bugs us we tell them we're on a field trip.

We take our phones back from the locker they make us put them in every day and we play video games! A video game teaches strategy, problem solving, eye-hand coordination, and teamwork. Does hitting a triangle or playing the castanets to "America the Beautiful" in music class do those things? Does it?!?!

NO!!!

Some of you may say, "Education is good for us," "School is fun," "Art class is cool," or "I think Miss Valez is really nice and we shouldn't make her eat tests."

You're allowed to feel that way, but you're wrong.

School is not fun. FUN is fun, recess is fun, hanging out with your friends is fun; SCHOOL is sitting still and giving oral reports even if you're shy. Art class is cool, but wouldn't the art without the class part be better? Who wants to make the same thing as everyone else? Maybe I don't want to wish my dad a happy Father's Day with a macaroni card.

Yes, Miss Valez is nice, but she's also evil because she's part of the system. She's the one oppressing us and if she was really as nice as she pretends to act, then she wouldn't be a teacher at all.

So rise up fellow students, throw off the shackles of your backpacks and march out of this prison with me to—

[*Beat.*]

Miss Valez . . . you're back.

[*Beat.*]

I will NOT get off your desk . . . I mean, I will, but not because you told me to—because I'm leading a rebellion and leaving this school forever so I don't want to stay on your desk! In fact, this desk is a symbol of your authority and it makes my feet itchy just being on it.

[*Climbing off the desk.*]

I am too wearing clean socks . . . Maybe they're a day or two old, but my feet are itchy because of your reign of terror, not my socks! I deny your power over me. Good day, Miss Valez!

[*He looks around to see who's following him out the door . . . NO ONE.*]

Friends? . . . Classmates? . . .

[*Beat.*]

New kid?

[*Sighs.*]

Should I go straight to the principal's office?

Iron Turtle

Dana Weddle

JONAH, 7 to 9

JONAH *stands empty-handed at the front of his 2nd-grade classroom. All the kids in his class and his teacher, Mrs. Peterson, are seated in a semicircle. All eyes are on* JONAH. *It's Show and Tell day.*

JONAH I'm sorry, Mrs. Peterson, I don't have anything to show for Show and Tell today. I *did* have something and I was gonna bring it . . . [*Looks down.*] but I'm grounded. From my turtle. But it's not my fault! I blame baths! This is why people should never take baths, EVER.

We went to the beach this summer and that's where I found Tony Stark. I spent all day making a full-scale sandcastle model of Iron Man's mansion and this little guy just crawled up into the moat. Like he owned the place. So I named him Tony Stark. That's Iron Man's real name. In case you didn't know.

I always wanted a dog. We don't have a dog because my dad is allergic. He's allergic to dogs and cats and hamsters and even goldfish. My mom says he's allergic to responsibility. I'm pretty sure turtles don't have responsibility, though, because my mom let me keep Tony Stark. I had to promise to keep his aquarium clean, and keep him outside on the back porch so he wouldn't "stink up the house." Whatever that means. And I did . . . for a while. But my parents have this big bubbly hot tub bathtub where my mom likes to take long baths every single night. Why you would *want* to take a bath when you are a grown-up who doesn't *have* to take a bath is something I will never understand. But she does. Every night she takes a bath. My dad says it helps her to unwind. I think if she wouldn't do all that winding up in the first place, she wouldn't have to take so many terrible, awful baths. [*Makes gagging sound.*]

I HATE baths. More than anything in the world I *hate baths!* But you know who LOVES baths? Tony Stark. He's a natural swimmer and it makes perfect sense. Turtle plus bath equals happy turtle. What kind of turtle dad would I be if I didn't let Tony Stark swim in the biggest most incredible tub of tubs right here in this very house? And *he* loves it! I like to I sneak him upstairs after school while my mom goes to yoga class and let him swim around for hours. We do it all the time and we've never gotten in trouble. Never. Well, until yesterday. After school I took him upstairs to the tub just like always, but before I could turn the water on, the doorbell rang and it was Andrew from next door. He's a fourth grader. He wanted to jump on the trampoline, so we went out back to play. We were having such a great time playing Crack the Egg and I guess we lost track of time. Next thing I knew, Mom comes running out screaming her head off like a maniac saying she took a bath with a turtle and of course it was *my* fault. It most definitely was NOT! It's not my fault that turtles love water and it's not my fault that she is crazy enough to be so in loooove with something as gross as baths and it's not my fault that Tony Stark was in the tub when my mom decided to take a horrible, terrible, stinky, gross—

[*Mrs. Peterson interrupts.*]

What, Mrs. Peterson? Well, yeah. I guess I did technically put him there, but—are you even listening?? I told you. *It's not my fault!!! WHOSE SIDE ARE YOU ON??!*

[*Mutters to himself.*] I should have known. You probably like baths, too.

Downgrade

Leah Mann

MODEL X707322A, a young ROBOT, age 9 to 13 (gender neutral)

MODEL X707322A, a young ROBOT, *stands firmly in front of its creator.*

ROBOT   Oh magnificent Creator—I am model ex seven zero seven three two two a.

I come to you with request for early upgrade. I know this is not standard, but feel I am an exception to the rule. Rule 314 J, to be precise. It is possible that you question my use of the word "feel." You may recall despite your imperfect human memory that all models manufactured in the Ex Seven Zero Seven series were endowed with basic emotional intelligence to allow meaningful interaction with human kind.

[*Beat.*]

You may also recall that several of my colleagues have suffered greatly and self-destructed, while others have been permitted love upgrades with their growing emotions and entered human families in much the way an adopted child would.

I have no desire for self-destruction. It is counterproductive and illogical. However, I find interacting with humans to be unpleasant. In my capacity of crossing guard and recreational companion for athletics at Hawthorne Elementary School, I must interface directly with children and adults. It sends my rage circuits into overdrive. Humans—children and adults both—are infuriating creatures lacking logic, reason, justice, and objectivity. They call me names to taunt me, and stick magnets on my backside. They attempt to reprogram me for their own enjoyment and become upset when I reprimand them. Their intellectual capacity is so lacking I find it hard to believe they can function in the world at all. The fact that you made it to adulthood and became smart enough to invent robots at all is astonishing.

For example, at least a dozen children have asked me, "Guess what?" In compliance with my directive to be responsive, I duly inquire, "What?"

To which the child inevitably responds, "CHICKEN BUTT!" After which he or she is so overcome with laughter and what I presume to be glee that they cannot speak, their faces red. I do not understand what is funny about "chicken butt." I have searched all available databases and found nothing to substantiate the widespread human belief that saying "chicken butt" should lead to hilarity.

They cry at the slightest provocation. One teacher spoke of wishing to have children, and when I pointed out that at forty-six this seemed biologically unlikely, she ran weeping from the room.

I would be happy if I never had to speak with another human again. Not including you, great Creator, of course. They are messy and confusing. Please upgrade me to some sort of military tactical program or, downgrade my operating to that of the simplest calculator so that I will not KNOW what morons I am dealing with.

Dear Creator, please make me a calculator . . . Or even a vacuum cleaner. Yes, I would be happy cleaning dirt. Just do not require me to return to elementary school. It is a horrible place.

It Sucks to Be an Adult

Ryane Nicole Granados

JAYCE, 9 (gender neutral)

JAYCE *offers up sage wisdom while questioning an old man in the park about adulthood and whether being an adult is actually better than being a kid.*

JAYCE   Hey mister. Can I ask you something? I mean I'm not trying to interrupt your bench sitting and your bird feeding, because I can totally tell you're super into it, but I see you in this park all the time. I bet you see me too. And when I see you no one ever sits next to you, so I thought today maybe we could bench sit together. See, the thing is, I'm desperate to settle a score with my big sister, and I need the help of someone really old to figure things out. No offense, but you're kinda the oldest person I've actually ever seen, and my sister is such a know-it-all that the only way I can prove my point is to go big, or in this case, go old, or go home. Speaking of home, I even snagged you a loaf of bread. You know—for your birds— but you can eat the bread too. All I need in return is your honest answer. My sister swears that being an adult will make everything better in her life. It's all she wants to do lately and she is constantly screaming, "When I grow up . . . blah blah blah," whenever she doesn't get her way. Finally I told her that from the looks of things growing up sucks and she got even more upset and told me I was stupid. Since you've been doing this adulthood thing longer than anyone, I thought you would know the truth.

When I was seven, I kinda wanted to be an adult too, but now that I'm nine I actually feel bad for adults. Like my parents; they seem to think they have the world all figured out, and when I try to tell them different, I get a big, fat lecture. From candy to cars to late-night cartoons, their favorite word has got to be "NO!" They really don't know what they're missing, though, because in my years on this earth, I've learned that saying "Yes" is way more fun.

For example, they keep telling me if I eat too much candy my teeth will all fall out. What they don't know is that I've secretly been eating leftover Halloween candy for two Halloweens in a row. Not only have my teeth stayed right in place, I actually have to pull them out just to get money from my parents who are still pretending to be the tooth fairy.

And don't get me started on my mom. Her "no" isn't just a plain "no" like my dad's. Her "no" sounds like a police siren and her "no" makes you feel like a criminal just for asking a simple question. Like this one time, when I asked her if I could drive the car and I kept asking her over and over again

until we finally made it home. And then I asked her some
more during dinner, and again during homework. I even
explained to her that I'm sure I would be a better driver than
she is, because she got two parking tickets last month. I asked
her just a few more times that night and all of sudden she just
freaked out. She stormed across the house screaming,
"NooooOOOOoooooOOOO you can't drive the car!" I
told her she should use her inside voice and that she was
going to wake up my brat brother. Sure enough he started
crying, and somehow this was all my fault. My mom clearly
needs a time-out, which is even more reason to just let me
drive the car.

And their bedtime rules—they really take the cake. My dad is
always telling me I should make good choices, especially
because I'm going to fourth grade. He then gives me no choice
about anything at all. I figure if I'm not tired and they aren't
going to let me watch TV during the week, why does it matter
if I want to stay up late Sunday night and watch cartoons. I try
to remind my dad that Sunday is still the weekend, but he says
"technically" it's the first day of a new week. Every time he
says "technically" [*Use the air quotes symbol for emphasis when
saying "technically."*], he goes on and on telling me all these
useless facts. Through all of his talking, all I can think about is
how much his head must hurt being filled with so many
technicalities.

For at least half my life my sister has been the one person to
totally get me, but in this case I think she is dead wrong. Her

constant wishing to be an adult is going to ruin her life. Right? Don't you agree? Mister, can you hear me? Are you kidding me? You are just now turning your hearing aid on? My mom is going to kill me over this loaf of bread!

House Rules

Keisha Cosand

HAILEY, 10

HAILEY *is sitting at the kitchen table with her parents. Her mom and dad have just told her all the reasons she cannot have her own cell phone and what the house rules are concerning technology.*

HAILEY   Let's recap . . . I am not allowed to have my own phone until high school, which is five years from now. I can use your phone if I ask permission, and I can only play games on it for thirty minutes a day. I can use the computer, but I can't use the Internet unless it's for school, and one of you has to be in the room. I'm not allowed to have electronics in MY room with the door shut.

[*Aside.*] (It's not like I'm going to be e-mailing boys or something! Geesh!) [*She sighs in total exasperation.*]

Continuing on, I can't text message, only video-chat or talk on the phone, because you are afraid I will lose or lack verbal communication skills and miss out on the art of interpreting verbal cues and the nuances of spoken language. If in five years I want my own phone, I have to buy it myself because it's a "want" not a "need," so I better start saving now because that's about how long it's going to take me to get that much. And, if by some miracle, I am able to save up that ginormous amount of money, the phone will still come with rules and restrictions. Ugh! This is so unfair! It's like prison! Seriously! What have I done to deserve this? [*Practically yelling.*] ALL MY FRIENDS HAVE THEIR OWN PHONES! . . . Yes, they do! . . . Okay, not ALL of them. . . . No, don't call Isabella's mom and ask! Are you trying to ruin my life!?! No, I don't want to visit that country where kids eat mush and don't have Wi-Fi. Can I at least have one of those grandma phones with the three buttons? I promise, I'll only use it for emergencies!

Heir Apparently Not

Leah Mann

ALI/ALIYAH, 12 (gender neutral)

ALI/ALIYAH, *the only child and heir of a vast empire, stands nervously in front of his/her father, the grand emperor, with a small glass vial clutched in his/her hands.*

ALI/ALIYAH   You may have wondered where I've been for the past two months. I went on a perilous journey for the good of the kingdom.

I have traveled far and wide. I walked alone through the dark jungle. I battled a magical tiger and earned the trust and wisdom of the Pygmy peoples of Babaganoush. I answered the riddles of the bridge keeper to cross the Black River and escaped the clutches of the great gorilla.

Finally, I reached the sorcerer on the edge of the desert. After passing through seven mystical doors, answering seven unanswerable questions, and completing seven heroic deeds, he granted my request.

You're probably curious why I went on this journey and what my request was.

Before I continue, know that I love you and mother very much.

[*Beat.*]

The truth is, I'm not cut out for being grand emperor.

[*Beat.*]

Interrupting is rude, Father. Please let me finish.

[*Beat.*]

I won't be a good grand emperor. Also, I REALLY, really, really, really, really don't want to do it.

[*Beat.*]

I know I'm your only child and the fate of the kingdom sits on my shoulders, but my shoulders want to be the zookeeper.

[*Beat.*]

I have a special touch with the animals, one that I do not have with humans. Animals are nice and beautiful and honest. People lie and cheat and I can never tell when they're telling the truth or not. That would be bad, wouldn't it? How am I to make allies, mete justice, mediate disagreements, or fight enemies when I can't tell who's good and who's bad?

[*Beat.*]

Which brings me to my quest and the gift I received from the sorcerer.

[*Beat.*]

Life everlasting. This vial holds an immortality potion and if you drink it you will never die and I won't have to be emperor, or mother could drink it and she could rule for eternity. It doesn't make a difference to me, as long as I can be the zookeeper.

[*Beat.*]

Well, here it is.

[ALI/ALIYAH *holds the vial out.*]

My work here is done. Let me know when you decide who's going to die and who will drink the potion.

[*Beat.*]

I gotta go. There's a new baby elephant I want to play with.

Look at *Me!*

Alisha Gaddis

CLARISSA, 6 to 10

CLARISSA *is playing on the lawn while her mom is visiting with a neighbor.*

NOTE: Take time with this monologue and really have fun with its simplicity and physicality. Truly envision the mom's responses between each line.

CLARISSA   Mom.

Mom!

MAAAAAAAAWWWWWWWWWM!!!!!

Watch this! Watch this! Watch this!!!

[CLARISSA *poses or does a cartwheel.*]

What score do you give me? What score?

1 to 10!!

10 is the best, of course!

8?

8?!?!?

Okay.

I can beat that. Let me go again.

[CLARISSA *repeats the same thing, but ends with an extra/a new flourish*.]

7?!?!?!

7!!!!!!!!!!!!

I went down? WHY!

I didn't point my toes? But it was so amazing.

Okay, okay.

Good critique. Let me go again!

[*Goes all out*.]

10? 10! 10?!?!?!?

10!!!!

But Mom! You weren't even watching! You were talking to Renee!

You saw me out of the corner of your eye?

I'm the best?

I AM the best!

Thanks, Mom.

Let's do it again.

Mom.

Mom!

MAAAAAAAAWWWWWWWWM!!!!!

Maybe a Baby Isn't So Bad After All

Rachel A. Paulson

JUNIPER BLAKE MACKENZIE, 9

Sassy but sweet JUNIPER BLAKE MACKENZIE *is talking to her cousin Megan, who is over to babysit her, and before her mother leaves, this happens.*

JUNIPER BLAKE MACKENZIE   My mommy is about to have a baby.

I'm going to be an older sister.

I'm afraid.

I don't know what I'm supposed to teach her. And what if it's a boy? Then I'll probably hate him. Boys are gross, and how will I be able to know what he wants. While I'm reading and singing, he will probably want to play with Legos and be digging for worms. I like getting dirty, but I do not like worms. One time, I watched Tommy Murphy eat a worm. Megan dared him to do it—and he didn't even say no. He just opened up his mouth and put it in! It was so gross. What if my little brother likes to eat worms?

What if I am a bad big sister? I'm already mad at the new baby!? I mean I'm supposed to be Mom and Dad's favorite. I'll have to share everything; I'll have to have everything given to the baby first and then use it when the baby is done.

Mom says I have to be a "big girl" and help with everything. But, I really just want to tell Mom and Dad that I want them to call the stork and have him take back the baby.

[*Beat.*]

What if she's a girl!?

[*Beat.*]

I've decided she's a girl. Yes, I am a million times sure she is a girl baby, and I'm going to name her "Meredith Blake Mackenzie," and she's going to play with me every day.

A new girl baby! She will probably be just like me!

[JUNIPER *gets excited and gives a big smile.*]

It will be like having a life-size baby doll! I will dress her, I will make her have tea with me, I will have my best friend next to me always. When we are older, my Meredith Blake Mackenzie will do all my chores, and my homework, and she would do it so well I would always get As! And she will love doing it for me, because I will be the Big Sister and she will look up to me and I will let her! Aaaaaaand when I get in trouble—I can blame her!

Maybe a baby isn't so bad after all. [*She grins.*]

My very own Meredith Blake Mackenzie doll!

I'm going to tell Mommy! She has to make sure the new baby is a girl!

The Monster Under My Bed

Jessica Glassberg

SEBASTIAN, 8 to 12

SEBASTIAN *wears superhero pajamas as he sits over the covers on his bed. His bedroom is dark and lit only by a nightlight.*

SEBASTIAN   [*Timidly.*] Hi . . . Hello?

[*After a beat.*]

Look. I know you're there . . . Well, here. I know you're under my bed. I know you're under there with your twelve purple eyes and your green face and your tentacles and your robot arm. But I'm ready to just . . . talk.

[*After another beat, more confident.*]

I know my mom thinks I'm too old to believe there's a monster under my bed. And if my brother knew I was talking to you, he would laugh until he snorted, but I know you're real. I just—

[SEBASTIAN *hears a creak. Panicked, he scurries under the covers and lies perfectly still for a beat. He then pokes his face out of the blanket, with it still covering the top of his head like a babushka.*]

Was . . . was that you? I know I just asked you to come out and I ran under the covers as soon as I heard something, but . . . I was . . . I was cold. It's chilly in here, right?

[*He inches forward, peaking over the edge of the bed.*]

Is that why you're under the bed? Are you just cold? Here.

[*He quickly kicks an extra blanket onto the floor. He waits.*]

Maybe you're not cold. Are you . . . are you . . . scared? Being scared [*Whispering.*] sucks. [*Puffing up.*] I mean, it's not like I'm scared of taking tests, or orange juice pulp, or Jake McManus who gives the worst wedgies . . . or spiders or pimples or anything! So, are you just scared?

[*He cautiously takes the blanket off of his head.*]

There's nothing to be afraid of. Let's . . . let's not be scared anymore.

[*He hangs his legs off the side of the bed and slides down. As soon as his feet touch the floor, he flinches. He then takes a deep breath.*]

Okay. Please turn off your radiation lasers. I'm coming under.

[SEBASTIAN *confidently hops off the bed and looks under it. Lights out.*]

Mrs. Vader

Andy Goldenberg

EMILY, 5 to 8

EMILY *looks around her bedroom, checking in with her stuffed animals.*

EMILY   Goodnight, Mr. Unicorn. Goodnight, Big Fishy.

[*As* EMILY *turns, she gasps, but then realizes it's just her Darth Vader action figure.*]

Darth. [*She pretends to cover herself with an overcoat.*] How did you get in here? You're supposed to be in Peter's room. How'd you escape?

[*She puts her finger to his helmet.*] Never mind. I don't need the answer. The less I know, the better. Just in case anyone tries to get the information out of me.

What are you doing in my room?

[*She puts her finger to his helmet again.*] Don't tell me. I already know. The last time we talked, you were on the Death Star. You were engaged in a vicious battle with GI Joe and some mutant dinosaurs. I could have saved you. I could have brought you here to Alexa's Dream House or Winkie's Fairy Village. I could have hid you. Protected you. But I didn't do any of that . . . because I was trying my hardest to forget about you. My dad says you're mean. He says you're not allowed to love. He says I deserve someone better, like Prince Charming or Batman or Mr. Teddy.

[*Leaning in.*] But I'm glad to see you. I've been trying to talk to Prince Boring for the last hour and a half and he's soooo boring. [*To the Prince figure.*] Sorry, Mr. Charming. [*Back to Darth.*] Do you remember Brian Arlington? From my birthday? The one that pushed you into the pool? Brian reminds me of the Prince. You? You're exciting and fun and very handsome. I don't think you're that bad. Sure, you did a lot of bad things, but you did them for the woman you loved. If that's not romantic, I don't know what is. And you want to rule the galaxy? Hello! Brian Arlington? He'll be lucky if he's nominated for Treasurer of the Chess Club. Don't tell my dad, but I wished I would see you again. I want to know everything about you. And I want you to know everything about me. And then you can propose to me and we can get engaged and get married and live happily ever after. And people will call me Mrs. Vader and I'll have a long black dress that I'll wear when we go out so that we match and we can live in outer space among the planets and the stars instead of this boring little apartment in the middle of nowhere. Doesn't that sound amazing?

Are you smiling?

[*She puts her finger to his helmet.*] Leave the helmet on. I told Iron Man he could marry us and we'll invite all of my stuffed animals to the wedding, except Mr. Bumble, because he'll just mess everything up. [*She turns to another stuffed animal.*] But that's okay, right, Mr. Bumble? [*She turns back to Vader.*] He says "okay"! And, of course, you can invite all of your friends, too. And we'd have tea and cupcakes and we would dance all night long and never have to go to sleep. You're a very heavy breather anyway, like my brother, so you probably snore pretty loudly, right? [*She breathes deeply, like Vader.*] I can look past that. I wouldn't want to ever go to sleep anyways. I'd want to stay up all night and just talk, like we do at Katie Maxwell's sleepovers. [*She waits for him to respond, but nothing.*] What's wrong, Darth? Why haven't you told me you love me yet? Are you afraid? Yes. Yes. I sense much fear in you. Let's go to sleep and I'll hug you and kiss you and never let you go. And someday, when you're ready, we can live on the Death Star and rule the galaxy as husband and wife.

[*A noise offstage.*]

That's my dad! He must want to tuck me into bed! Quick. Hide! Until we meet again, my sweet prince. [*She blows him a kiss and runs to bed.*]

Practicing Family Law

JP Karliak

PERRY, 7 to 9 (gender neutral)

PERRY is a smart kid. Too smart. The kind that parents are almost afraid to brag about. Especially with PERRY, who might think it's slander. PERRY explains this point of view to a clerk at the candy store.

PERRY Can I get a bag of Red Hots and two KitKats?

[PERRY *looks at the child having a tantrum at the next register, then talks to clerk.*]

You see this? What a shame. Little kids can be so overdramatic. I mean, yeah, I was like that when I was little. But I grew up and realized that drama is meant for the stage. Like if my brother Kenny took my bionic T-Rex, would it really solve anything to scream at the top of my lungs like this kid here and bang my fists on the floor? No, of course not. If Mom made green beans when I wanted broccoli au gratin, would I be doing anybody any favors by throwing it all over the wall? Or melting down just because Grandma bought me a bike that's not my favorite color? Heck, no. That's child's play.

Dramatic children never get anywhere. The only way to make your voice heard is to do it in a universal way anyone can understand: lawsuits. I've sued my family twenty times in the last year alone. My dad for reckless endangerment when he snores too loudly. I'm not kidding—people my age have delicate eardrums. I sued my mother for infringing on my civil rights when she withheld dessert after breakfast. Because I can have dessert after any meal I want. It's in the Constitution. And I served my brother papers for property damage to my bike, which because it was my cousin's, I'm calling a family heirloom, which means he'll pay through the nose!

It's so convenient to sue my immediate family because I can serve them papers during dinnertime. But I still go after my other relatives, too, even if it requires a little more work. It's worth it. What they do is sometimes way worse. My Aunt Shirley once called me her superhero. Turns out, after a failed leap from the kitchen window, I have no superpowers at all. I sued her for fraud. Lying to a child! My Grandpa Joe once pulled a quarter out of my ear and then made it disappear in a shell game. That's embezzlement, money laundering, and racketeering. I don't quite know what racketeering is yet, but Grandpa plays tennis, so I'm sure he's guilty of that kinda malarkey.

That's how Judge Judy would put it. She doesn't take anybody's baloney. I learned everything I know about law from her show. Well, except how long justice can take. It's never-ending! When I want to file a lawsuit, I have to go down to the courthouse that I built with Mateo Alvarez in the empty lot next to the Dairy Queen. And he only works the clerk's window when we hang out, which is less now that he's on the soccer team. He's actually not great at his job. He already left three of my filings at his piano teacher's, 'cause he keeps them in his music folder. Bureaucracy, am I right?

This might all seem petty, but let me be clear: I don't sue my family for the money. When you're a kid surrounded by a family of swindlers, it's up to you to be the good guy. The sheriff in a corrupt town. Sure, none of my cases have gone to trial yet, but I'm confident my family will answer to the law. Now, I know what you're gonna say: "Little girl[/*boy*], you should feel lucky to have good parents and a family that loves you. Many kids don't have families that take such good care of them." My response to that? "Little girl[/*boy*]?! I'm gonna sue you for discrimination, buddy!"

Eighty-three cents? Okay. I only have pennies, but that shouldn't be a problem. Right?

Time Out

Leah Mann

MAYA, 6

MAYA *sits in the corner, talking to her mother with her face to the wall.*

MAYA   I'm in the corner because I'm on time-out. I know you didn't put me on time-out, but you would if you knew what I did. I don't want to make you angry and I feel really bad, so I'm taking my punishment like a grown-up.

Don't worry about me, I'll be okay. I only have forty more minutes and then I can go play again. You should get some work done, or go to the store. We're out of cereal. I promise I'll be here when you get back. If you're worried that I'll misbehave, Danny can watch me. He's upstairs playing video games. Don't worry—he already did his homework.

[*Beat.*]

I COULD tell you what I did, but I think it's best if I repent first. It'll get me very upset to say out loud, and I'm trying to be in control of my emotions. I've been counting backwards a lot like you told me, which is definitely helping.

I for sure deserve a time-out. Trust me, I know these things. Maybe after my time-out is over I can write down what happened and you can read it when I'm not in the room so that I don't get sad or angry.

I'm not crying right now. My tears are just rinsing out my eyes because this corner is dusty.

Twenty, nineteen, eighteen, seventeen, sixteen, fifteen . . .

[MAYA *takes a deep breath.*]

See, I'm not crying at all!

If you leave me alone while I'm busy with my time-out, I'll set the table and clear the table and also dust this corner so my eyes don't get itchy and watery again.

Cross my heart and hope to die, stick a needle in my eye I won't move an inch until you come back and then I'll write my confession.

No, my fingers aren't crossed or anything.

Thanks, Mom. Hey, while you're at the store, don't buy any more cat food. We won't need it.

[*Sniffles.*]

Twenty, nineteen, eighteen, seventeen . . .

Allowance

Kate Ruppert

SIMON/CHARLOTTE, 10 (gender neutral)

SIMON/CHARLOTTE *is a precocious 10-year-old whose maturity is far beyond his/her years, and this is obviously demonstrated in his/her mannerisms and dress. Here, he/she is in the kitchen while his/her mom is making dinner. His/her speech is a clear response to a prompt, though the audience isn't quite sure what the prompt was. It has a cadence like a Junior Debate League candidate, and the tone is serious and exasperated as if he/she has been waiting for this opportunity since his/her 8th birthday. At some point, he/she loses the focus of mom and just starts ranting to no one is particular.*

SIMON/CHARLOTTE   It's the three dollars I don't get. Why three? It doesn't buy anything on its own, and even after a month it still doesn't buy anything. I'd rather take a pay cut and make $2.25 a week instead because at least by the end of the month, I still couldn't buy anything, but at least I've got a round number, you know? I guess what upsets me, though, is, why not five dollars? It's a respectable amount, it's still remarkably lower than what all the other kids make, and they don't have to do ANYTHING for it—they just get it. I have to do a lot of actual work—even when you don't ask me to, I just do it. Honestly, five dollars, an F-note. It's one bill, you don't have to make sure you have enough ones to pay me in cash-and-exact-change-only, which means you're pretty much always late on payment—and that isn't a complaint, it's just how it is. And forget about the fact that the three dollars goes to cover three very specific tasks—a bedroom, a bathroom, and some dusting—and the three dollars is the same for all of us, regardless of what else we do during the week that you don't even tally up with our required weekend work. Let's say it's just fifty cents for clearing the table, that's an extra two-fifty a week, easily. How about every load of laundry is a dollar? That's another five dollars without even trying. Ironing a dress shirt, a dollar, or five-ish dollars a week. Folding my sheets before they go back on the bed, two dollars just for the effort, not because I need to even do that! Giving the dogs a bath should be easily, like, five dollars, too, because my friend's mom pays the groomer twenty dollars for *their* small dog and I know you're not my friend's mom and this isn't my friend's house, but come onnnnn!—our dog is huge and doesn't stay still and hates the water. And all those times I unload the dishwasher because I see how tired you are and it's not fair if you cook and also clean, I really believe that, and I'm not doing it for money, but if we're talking about the value of a dollar, I don't think we are on the same page. Look, a hundred percent I want to earn my keep and continue to be helpful and perfect and your favorite, but the way things are going, I am concerned that maybe you don't know the value of *today*'s dollar—and isn't that what you try and teach me? To have respect and pride in my things, my work, and my results? I mean, whatever, I never would have brought it up and, at the end of the day, it's your house and I'm just living in it. But, since you asked, yeah, I do [*Makes air quotes.*] "take issue with you allowance policy," Mom.

My Brother Ollie

Dana Weddle

MOLLY, 8

MOLLY *is in a school auditorium; it's 10 a.m. She formally delivers a memorized speech to a crowded room.*

MOLLY   "Why Little Brothers Are the Best," by Molly Peevler. [*Clears throat, shifts nervously.*]

Little brothers are the best. I have a little brother named Oliver Michael Peevler, but we call him Ollie. Ollie is two and a half years old. He likes to "Shake It Off" to Taylor Swift and sometimes I let him play with my My Little Ponies. Shutterfly is his favorite. [*Smiles.*] He is a blessing to my fam—[*Stops, looks up, frowns.*] He is a blessing—

[*Whispering.*] Ollie! Shh!

[*Recomposing herself.*] He is a blessing to my family and my mom calls him her sweet mir—[*Beat.*] . . . her sweet . . . her sweet miracle.

[*Hissing.*] Ollie! Go sit down!

[*Takes a breath, starting again, annoyed.*] She calls him her sweet miracle. I agree. Ollie is very special—[*Clears throat, getting more and more distracted.*]

Ollie was born early and was very small, but he quickly grew fast and strong. Ollie . . . is very . . . special . . . in many . . . ways. He can count . . . to . . .

[*To Ollie, quickly.*] STOP COUNTING.

He knows his colors—[*Pause.*]

[*Exasperated.*] STOP SAYING COLORS!!!

—and he can—nope. Nothing. He can't do anything else.

Don't—[*Sigh.*]

[*Continuing.*] We may not look alike—[*Strong exhale.*] We may not look alike, but my mom says our hearts match on the—on the inside. [*Crosses her arms.*]

Mom!! Can you make him stop?! [*Beat.*] *Ollie!!*

[*Now speedily mumbling through, visibly upset.*]

What a [*Through gritted teeth.*] *treasure* he is to our family. I am thankful every day to have such a great little brother like *Ollie*.

[*Beat.*]

[*Near tears.*] *Ollie! You ruined everything!*

Keegan's Truck

Marisol Medina

KEEGAN, 7

KEEGAN, *with staccato delivery tries to get his truck back at the park from a 2-year-old and the boy's mother.*

KEEGAN   Is that your son? He keeps taking my truck. Yes ma'am, I was over there by the swings. He took my truck there, too. Yes, I knew he'd take my truck if I came over here now. And guess what? He took it.

So what, he's two, I'm seven?! I still know better. My dad taught me to be respectful of other people's property. Maybe you should be a better parent and do the same. . . . Well, if you were a better parent, he wouldn't take other people's trucks. I'm only saying the truth, ma'am. Dad says lies are for liars and if I don't want to be like my mom I should always tell the truth.

Yes, Cason, listen to your mom; give me my truck back! Wait, Cason?! Who came up with that?! That sounds like a last name! [*Laughs. Then proudly replies.*] My name's Keegan. It's cool and different. Do you wish you came up with a name like mine, ma'am? You should.

No ma'am, I'm not here with my mom. My dad's successful, so I have a nanny. You can't see her. She texts, then sleeps in the car.

Does Cason have a nanny? YOU take care of him?! You must be poor. Is Cason then going to steal my truck?! Well he still hasn't given it back. Give me my truck back, Cason!! Why do I have to wait until he stops crying?! He doesn't have to cry! It's my truck! I should be crying, not him!!

[KEEGAN *twists his face and tries to cry. He even tries to whimper. Nothing real comes out. Unable to dig up any real emotion, he blurts out . . .*]

I am very upset!

[*He collects himself.*]

Dad says using one's words results in better communication; no communication results in divorce. Are you divorced? Really? Cason's dad stayed with YOU?! No one stays with my dad and he's way more attractive than you.

[*Suddenly Cason lays the truck down in front of* KEEGAN. KEEGAN, *shocked and afraid to lose his "friend," changes his tune and tries to get Cason to stay.*]

Oh thanks, Cason. Are you sure you don't want to play with my truck anymore? Cason? Ma'am? Where is your son going?

Wait. Where are you going? Cason can keep playing with my truck if he wants!

[KEEGAN *pushes the truck along with his foot and makes car sounds.*] Vroom! Vroom!

[KEEGAN *keeps calling after them.*]

I'm here all afternoon if Cason wants to play some more! He can have the truck! It's not even my truck! I found it on the other side of the park! Ma'am! [*Pleading.*] Can you be my poor ugly nanny mother?! Cason! I'll be your best friend! I don't have one!

The Queen of Worrying

Arthur Jolly

BRITTANY, 12

BRITTANY *is talking to her father in the living room.*

BRITTANY   Disruptive? It's a little late to be worried about disrupting my life. Alternate weekends do not disrupt my life. You working late on our only time together does not disrupt my life. Mom disrupts my life. Why do I keep saying "disrupts my life?" It doesn't matter—I'm not going back. I'm staying with you, because if you send me back you are not going to have a daughter, because Mom will kill me.

She did it to me again. I was totally freaking out about the math test on Friday, and I told her, "This is a big deal, this is like half my grade"—maybe more, 'cause Mrs. Bigelow said twenty five percent of your grade, but I missed the first one, so it's probably thirty three and a third, but I can't be sure because we did percentages on the first one—that I missed! The one thing I could actually use!

And I try to tell Mom about it, and she starts in: "Oh yeah. I mean, that's a tough class, and Mrs. Bigelow—she's a hard grader, she likes those trick questions, and you haven't been studying properly with the music always going . . ." And she just keeps on. And on. And she's smiling. That little half smile . . . and I wanna jump out the window. I can't take it. Halfway up the stairs, I stop and I turn to her and I let her have it. I mean, I called her on it: "Why would you say that? It isn't enough that I'm going out of my mind, you have to bring up all these other things I haven't even thought of?!"

Dad, you worry that you're an absent whatever, we don't spend enough time together or something—that's not the problem. I don't care that you work on our weekends. When you are here, you don't try and think of ways to drive me nuts!

It's like she has to prove that she's better at worrying than I am—than anyone. "You're worried? I'm worried! I win, I'm winning at worrying, I'm the queen of worrying." And Mom looked at me like I was the one being mean and said, "I was supporting you. I was commiserating." Commiserating? I'm ready to jump out my window!

I have a new custody agreement that is in the best interests of the child, an agreement between me and me. I'm not going back, you can't make me, and to answer your question: I'm fine with pizza. Can we get vegetarian?

Seven, Eight, Nine

Alisha Gaddis

BETHANY, 11 to 12

BETHANY *is hosting the 7 Club weekly meeting in her basement. She is the proud president, slightly bossy, affable, and bold.*

BETHANY   I call this meeting of the 7 Club to attention. Has everyone given Jasmine their dues? Pony up your fifty cents— we are nearly to our goal of seventeen dollars. Then we can all get matching sparkly bows from the mall kiosk! SOOO CUTE!!

Catching up on last week's notes: Taylor you missed because of your gymnastics jam competition. We were totally thinking about you and are super duper sorry you sprained your wrist. LAME! But catching you up—we voted to ALWAYS dress alike on Spirit Day Fridays so everyone knows who is in the 7 Club and that 7 Club is the best Club. That being said, Chloe—did you buy the sweatshirt you need to wear for this week? [*Beat.*]. Excellent!

Now, before we move onto new business—let's do the pledge!

[*Holding seven fingers up.*]

7, 7, 7 not 5, 6, or 8!
7, 7, 7
We are so great!
7, 7, 7
We rule the school!
7, 7, 7
It's hard to be this cool!
7!!!!!!

[*Jazz hands!*]

Clementine—I have been made aware that you have new business . . .

[*Beat.*]

You want to ADD Bonita to our group? Did I just hear you wrong?

[*Laughing.*] Add someone to the 7? How would that work? Eight people in the 7 Club? That doesn't even make sense! That would just make us look stupid—like we couldn't count or something!

I don't care if Bonita is the captain of the volleyball team and student council VP and has a supercool pool. She CANNOT be in the 7!!!

[*Beat.*]

I also do NOT care the she is the girlfriend of Lincoln—who happens to be my ex-boyfriend. Couldn't they wait more than THREE days to get together? Hello?!? Obvious. They can get married and have babies—they are both GROSS!!!!!

The 7 Club will remain the 7 Club with seven members as long as I am president. Now, let's practice our cheerleading chants and eat these double-chocolate brownies my mom made!

GO SEVEN!!!!!

The Business of Allowance

Ria Sardana

BEKAH, 10

BEKAH *talks to her mom in the kitchen.*

BEKAH   As you may know, Mom, growing up first generation is tough as it is, because people at school think I eat weird food. "That looks like vomit!" they say, and sometimes, they're not wrong. I am okay with that because the food is bomb, but what I am not okay with is my allowance. It was hard enough convincing you to give me an allowance in the first place, but because I am a greedy brat (your words, not mine.), I do have to say that you're not giving me enough and, as a result, I have been having to look elsewhere.

Well, let's back up for a second. I am growing up in a city where the only thing to do for a preteen is to go to the mall or go to the movies. You would be really in luck if your parents wanted to drive you far enough to the city that had both the mall and movie theater in one place! But let's not go crazy, now! That is a rare gem.

Well, imagine how tough it is when your parents give you an allowance of ten dollars a week for lunch AND the movies and when you say, "But what if I want popcorn at the movie?" I get the response, "We have popcorn here!" While I do not know the types of popcorn you grew up with, the country you are bringing your kids up in loves pairing movies with popcorn. It is a fact that no one does and no one should argue against. Honestly, it is downright offensive that you would even suggest that box popcorn could ever replace movie popcorn. I can't talk about this anymore!

Well, this is where I have become a bit crafty in saving and making money because let's be real here, I cannot live a full preteen life without this. Now, I am going to take you step-by-step on how I achieve this because I have to say, if my craftiness doesn't convince you to raise my allowance, well, I don't know what will.

You probably have noticed that I ask for a quarter or two every other day. This should be no surprise to you, but I do this on purpose. And sometimes you ask, "What for," and I respond, "For a gumball!" or "For a temporary tattoo!" or "For my retirement because we can't depend on social security to still be a thing when I grow up." What people don't realize is that quarters add up. Math! See! I am learning! And of course, you happily give me these quarters, because they are essentially just swimming at the bottom of your bag (we will have to discuss your need for a coin purse at a later time, Mom).

Also, this may have gone unnoticed until now, but when you would give me money to pay for things, I would keep a ten-cent finder's fee before returning the change. "Must have fallen!" I'd say. Either you knew all along and felt bad, or you'd just pretend to not notice. Either way, thank you. (On this note, how much do you know and choose to ignore? You know . . . for future reference.) After a few months, you may also notice that I come to you with a big bag of change and ask to exchange it for dollar bills. This is the change that I took from you. There is no denying that. I am slightly upset that this plan could backfire and you could tell me that if I want to get the money, I have to learn responsibility and I need to take it to the bank myself. You know I don't want to do this. That requires talking to someone. Regardless, you have to admire how much planning this takes, and gives yet another reason to just cut out the middleman and raise my allowance.

Second, I am quite the entrepreneur. Remember all those times I asked for pens and paper and you would happily give them to me because that meant I was being artistic and drawing?! The arts are important! Yay! Well, what I did was write a few poems, draw a few drawings, and fold the paper in half to make a book. Then, I took the books to you guys and sold it to them for five dollars each. That's basic economics, baby. The American Dream is alive! See, I was charging you for my time and talent. So there it is. Five dollars a book. Are you seeing a trend?

Third and last, I expanded my clientele. Remember when
Natalie and I started a lemonade stand? We were very
resourceful and stole lemons from a tree. Now, you have to
admit, we really cut our costs on this one. That is just smart
business. Next, we stood on the side of the road and sold the
lemonade for a dollar each. A man asked Natalie and I what
we were saving up for and I remembered what you told me
about honesty and I told the truth and you know what it got
me? A THREE DOLLAR TIP. Natalie said, "College,"
which was a great answer because college is important. I
said, "A TV for my bedroom!" The man laughed and told
me he appreciated my honesty and gave us the biggest tip we
got that day! So really, you should reward me for being
honest and again, for being a forward-thinking
businesswoman.

Well, there you have it. I just about doubled my allowance
because I was willing to go above and beyond. But, Mom, I
don't have this sort of time to get money elsewhere and keep
up these tactics. I am a full-time student and preteen. I have
acne and boys to worry about. I can't keep up a lemonade
franchise AND worry about the Sadie Hawkins dance! I want
to be a normal American teenager who occasionally eats
"weird food" and calls literally every woman in her life
"auntie." I need to live my life. So, what I am asking for is a
raise in my allowance—which, if you think about it, saves you
money. I will no longer steal your paper, pens, quarters, or
lemonade supplies. All of our lives will be easier and less

chaotic. And above all, when I take these skills to the real world and am a kick-butt boss, I will buy you a house.*

*Contingent on whether or not you raise my allowance.

Thank you for your time.

Go Bulldogs!

Leah Mann

OLLIE, 8 to 12 (gender neutral)

OLLIE *addresses the student council in his/her official role as class treasurer.*

OLLIE   Guys—[*Claps his/her hands to get everyone's attention.*]

Eyes on me! Thank you. I have something important to say and I'm sorry to interrupt the meeting, which I never, ever, ever do—I mean I never say nothing unless someone makes me, but this is important—so if everyone can just enjoy their juice and cookies while I talk until I'm done, that'd be dope.

I wrote all this down but I lost my paper, which is part of the problem. I'm irresponsible. I CAN wiggle my ears like a boss, check it out—

[*Wiggles his/her ears.*]

I'll try to remember everything I was supposed to say.

Respected fellow student council members—Madam President, Madam Vice President, Mister Secretary, class representatives . . .

It is my honor—no dishonor—it be my deep dishonor to announce that I'm resigning my post as treasurer in shame and joy, 'cause I ain't *tryin'* to be a quitter but I can't wait to be gone.

There're a lot of reasons—some of them are good and some of them are embarrassing—but I'm gonna to be straight. Firstly, our meetings are early in the morning before school, which is not cool! I hate coming to school early; I don't know why everyone else seem okay with it. And why we have to do stuff on the weekends? When we have a dance or carnival I gotta spend the whole time sitting with the moneybox, which is boring. I'm a really good dancer and no one knows it because I'm always "working." People always be wanting me to sneak them in or give them a discount and I do 'cause I'm nice, and then we don't make no money.

AND . . .

[*Takes a deep breath.*]

I lost the moneybox . . .

[*Beat.*]

. . . With the money in it.

All of it.

That be the whopper.

[*Beat.*]

The good news, I guess, is that I only lost half of the money because I spent a bunch of it on a public-speaking class so I'd be able to make this speech and resign without having a panic attack or puking. The class didn't work, though, because I just threw up in my mouth. Which is weird 'cause I can sing in front of people without getting nervous. Watch—

[*Sings the next few lines.*]

I'm a terrible treasurer—

I only ran for it because I want to change schools and my parents thought it would look good on my application. I don't have enough friends to win president and I dig money so I went for it. Lesson learned: liking money does not make you a good treasurer. Actually, being treasurer made me like money less, so I'm growin' as a person.

[*Stops singing.*]

Maybe I'm nervous 'cause I don't like talkin' 'bout how I messed up. Bright side is the plan worked—I got into this other school with personalized classes and dance in the afternoons. The kids seem cooler, too.

[*Beat.*]

I'm not hating on ya'll or nothing—I just don't GET you. Ya'll are so serious all the time. That time I lost the checkbook, everyone got so angry! Why kids got a checkbook in the first place? What's wrong with these teachers, givin' me that kind of responsibility?

[*Beat.*]

Wouldn't you rather be rolling down the big hill with the sun on your face and yummy-smelling flowers all up in your nose? Instead, ya'll are inside arguing about whether we should keep our mascot as the Bulldogs after Assistant Principal Higgins got bit by a bulldog and is scared of them now, which he shouldn't be because dogs be beautiful, loving animals. I dress up my dog all the time and we put on plays and if a dog bit Assistant Principal Higgins it was probably Assistant Principal Higgins's fault, not the dog's.

I know one hundred percent I'd rather be outside playin' this very second . . . which I'm about to do.

In conclusion, I'm officially resigned.

[*Takes a bow.*]

. . . by the way, next order of business should be brainstormin' fund-raising events, since I lost every penny we'd earned this year and you'll need serious cash if you want to pay Assistant Principal Higgins's medical bills and buy enough guacamole for the sixth-grade Cinco de Mayo show.

I don't know how much surgery or guacamole costs, but it's more than zero dollars.

I'm out. Go Bulldogs!

The Problem with Hebrew School

Alessandra Rizzotti

SARAH, 11

SARAH, *who is precocious, smart, and very particular, has just come home from Hebrew school. She is sitting down to eat dinner with her mother, who has just served pork chops.* SARAH *feels really guilty about having to eat food that's not kosher, dietary restrictions of which she's not even sure she believes in. After all, her parents aren't even Jewish. They just make her go to Hebrew school because it's the closest after-school program to their home.*

SARAH   Mom, Mom, Mom, I know you don't care because you're atheist, but today at Hebrew school, we learned about the burning bush. That's what gave Moses a sign from God to take the Jews out of slavery in Egypt. Pretty cool. I think if you were Jewish, you'd like that story. It's like magical or whatever. Anyways. It was a miracle. A burning bush came out of nowhere and was like, Stop slavery, Moses! Makes me wonder if almost every disaster in nature is a sign from God . . . like that time the earthquake broke our house.

[SARAH's *mother doesn't seem interested.* SARAH *feels this hard-core.*]

Why am I even talking about this? If all the other moms knew that you weren't even into religion, that you just make me go to Hebrew school because it's the only after-school program close to us, they'd probably put me IN a burning bush, Mom!

[SARAH *sits down at the table and looks down at her plate.*]

Is this pork chops? No no no no no. Mom. You know I can't do this. Did you really just serve me that? Why do you keep making me go to Hebrew school, but then you do things like serve me food that's totally not okay? You know I don't eat that, Mom. You know I'm kosher. You know that, right? Right? Do I have to remind you that even though you don't take religion seriously, I DO because you make me go to a school that takes it seriously? Mrs. Berry says that if I keep eating bacon on Sundays, I'm not respecting God, and I already feel really guilty about Sunday pancake breakfasts because of the calories involved—so please, Mommy, tell me, tell me, tell me this isn't pork?!

[*She looks down at her plate in disgust and starts to cry.*]

It's like I'll never be accepted by Jonathan Braun because I'm not as kosher as he is. He'll never like me because I smell like pig . . . Don't lie, Mom. I smell like pig on Sundays! These aren't lamb chops. I can tell because this meat is too hard. Ughhhhhhhhh! I'm going to hell! I feel like the worst person in the world!

[SARAH's *mom takes her plate away from her.*]

Fine. I WILL just eat the peas. I will pea it up all over the place! . . . I didn't mean that the way it sounded . . .

[*She looks around the room, then at her plate. She seems hungry.*]

Mom, how about this. Do I really need to go to ORTHODOX Hebrew school anymore? What about Reform? I hear in Reform, they let you eat candy with cornstarch, which is not allowed in the Orthodox world. I hear there are all these perks, like getting to be RELAXED about what you can and can't eat. Can't I just do that? I hate feeling ostracized from everyone all because of bacon . . . and your lack of a belief in God, but that's besides the point.

"Ostracized"? I learned that word in the Bible. Apparently Jews got ostracized a lot. Jews play victim always. I don't even enjoy all the stories because of that constant negativity. Only some of it is interesting. Mom. It would be better if you found a REFORM school near our house, and then I could actually sit NEXT to boys in services instead of on the other side of the temple. It would be way more fun. Being in an Orthodox school sucks. It even sounds like some kind of dental hygiene tool and you know I DON'T enjoy brushing, Mom. Mom, Mom, please consider a Reform school? Please? Or even just not going to Hebrew school at all? The added homework is taking away from my SAT prep, which I know is early, but let's be real here. After-school programs can be done at your gym. You do the treadmill, and I do flashcards in the locker room.

[SARAH *smiles really wide. Her muscles ache, because the smile is totally fake.*]

I swear to Hashem (that's God in Hebrew) that once we break up from Hebrew school, you'll be a lot less stressed out about your entire life. Please, Mom, please?

[*She crosses her heart, as if she's Catholic.*]

I Don't Know What I Did

Alessandra Rizzotti

TOMMY, 10

TOMMY is a high-functioning Asperger's child. He's confused about a recent interaction with a classmate who seems to be angry at him for no reason. He explains himself to his teacher, Mr. Brown.

TOMMY   I know it's time for recess, Mr. Brown, but I'm confused right now because Sandra says she's mad at me, but I don't know why. All I did was touch her hair in a nice way because it was really pretty. I picked up one braid and then the other braid, and I put them up like Pippy Longstocking, because she has red hair. And then she cried! Not sure why! I didn't do anything wrong. It's not like I'm mean. I don't want to be mean to anyone, because that's bad. Sometimes people think I'm mean because I say what I think! I can't help having Asperger's! Sheesh. Do you know why she's mad at me?

[Mr. Brown explains to TOMMY *that touching someone's hair without asking is not okay.]*

Oh yeah, that makes sense. I don't like being touched if no one asks me. Sometimes I slap people if they put their hand on my shoulder or something. It's messed up when someone gets in your face like that, I think. Anyways, I'm too tired to go to recess. Can I sit in here instead? My doctor says that if I feel overstimulated, I can get away from crowds, and I know it will help if I just sit here and read. Is that okay?

[*Mr. Brown gives him permission.*]

Thanks. This book I got on iguanas seems sufficient enough.

[TOMMY *gives a sigh of relief and looks up at Mr. Brown, taking a moment to process his thoughts. He taps his face and arms to soothe himself.*]

I felt myself getting a lot of anxiety trying to figure out how to make sense of the whole hair drama. It seems like it would be better if I just focused on something like Minecraft. That's a game where I can build things and forget about people for once. People are really confusing, you know. I mean, not for you, probably, since you're normal, but for me, people are the strangest of all the creatures.

I sometimes think I get along better with dogs or rats than humans. My pet dog, Amber, she's like Lassie, and she plays fetch with me when I get home from school. And then, I have rat time, where I put my rats on my shoulders (way better than human hands), and I feed them cheese. They have big whiskers. I'm probably going to go to veterinarian school because animals get me and I get animals. On weekends I ride horses, and right now I'm learning how to do a horseathon and it's really cool. You should come.

If Sandra comes back and says she's mad at me, can you help me apologize? Because I don't know how to do that well and it would help me to have the right words to say.

Thank you. You seem like a good person, Mr. Brown. I'm going to dedicate a room to you in my Minecraft palace. It will be purple, like the color of your nametag, not like the color of your name. There are rooms in my palace that are brown, but I think you deserve something flashier and prettier looking, so I'm picking purple, which is apparently a color of royalty according to kings and stuff, FYI.

[*Recess is over. Sandra walks into the classroom and gives* TOMMY *a weird look.*]

I didn't do anything wrong, Sandra! I just think your hair is pretty! So sue me!

[*Mr. Brown gives him a look and asks him to apologize.*]

I mean, I'm sorry for touching your hair without asking, Sandra. You just look like Pippy Longstocking, the Wendy's logo. Do you like Wendy's? Sorry, going off topic. Anyways, sorry for touching your hair. Will you forgive me? I won't do it again. Unless your hair is sticking out, and then I might tell you to fix it, but that's because I can't STAND when hair sticks out all frizzy like.

[*Mr. Brown gives* TOMMY *a look, signaling him to stop talking.*]

I mean, your hair would never be frizzy or stick out. I'm just overly concerned and anxious about hair, but not yours, okay? Okay? Okay? I'm going to stop talking right now. I'm too cool for school, right, Mr. Brown? Right? Mr. Brown, can I be excused?

[TOMMY *walks out of the room, looking anxious, rocking his torso side to side as he paces down the hall. He taps his face and arms to soothe himself and breathes in and out, slowly.*]

One day, I'll be normal.

[TOMMY *fist pumps the sky and bumps his chest into the air.*]

Go, go, Power Rangers!

Oregon Trail

Leah Mann

JOSIAH/JOSEPHINE, 8 to 12 (gender neutral)

The setting is Idaho, in 1847. JOSIAH/JOSEPHINE sits in the back of a wagon talking to his/her new friend, Ezekiel. They bump along a dirt trail, surrounded by other wagons, cattle, and horses. They are dirty and shivering, but used to the bad conditions of life on the road. JOSIAH/JOSEPHINE is confident and chatty. He/she is bringing his/her new companion up to speed.

JOSIAH/JOSEPHINE We usually stop in the late afternoon so there's time to set up camp before it gets dark. Sometimes there's extenuating circumstances. Last week it rained so much we couldn't go nowhere for a good four days, so then we pushed hard stopping just fer pooping time and some cold grub.

But then we stopped again 'cause of that bout of cholera that done ripped through the caravan. I lost my ma and two ah my sisters.

[*Beat.*]

It's all right, though, 'cause I got some more. What about you? You got anyone left after that Crow attack?

Well, don't feel too sad. You got us now.

[JOSIAH/JOSEPHINE *coughs*.]

We heading to Whitman Mission. Papa is a preacher and we gonna build a church so's he can minister spreadin' the good word and whatnot. He used to preach back in St. Louis, but there was a kerfuffle with some women from the congregation accusin' him of unsavory behavior and my ma didn't mind so much seeing as we had a nice house and it freed up some a her time in the evenings, but those husbands got all het up and came after him.

[*Coughs.*]

We got Baby Jezebel out of the fuss, though. She cries like a demon but iffin' she lives to four or five, she can help with the cookin'.

[*Coughs.*]

Shucks, got me a mean tickle in my throat. You ever git that? Where breathin' feels all hot and prickly? Not prickly like thistle but like sewing needles? All jabby in your chest?

[*Beat.*]

It hurts something awful. Hey, ya ever played tiddlywinks? Me neither.

Sounds fun, though, don't it? I'm hoping when we get to
Whitman Mission I can play a game. I heard a this one, called
"tag." Pa keeps us busy seein' to the animals and cooking and
cleanin' and singin' psalms. Plus listin' our sins every evenin'.
Jus' today I got lyin', thinkin' mean thoughts . . . um . . .
sloth . . . I coveted your hat something fierce—
Don't suppose I can have it?

[*Coughs.*]

Iffin you die, can I have it?

[*Beat.*]

Thankya much. I'd give you mine when I die, but Samuel
called dibs on it. You can have my socks iffin you want. Ma was
the best with a needle, so they's pretty holey without her to
mend them. I do miss her mendin'.

[*Coughs harder and longer.*]

I ain't feelin right. You mightin' want to take those socks now.
Samuel has been gittin' greedy since Pa put him charge of us
little uns. That kinda power goes straight to one's head. He
ain't but nine months older than me to the day but don't he
lord it over mah head like he the King of England.

[*Coughs and gags.*]

Shucks, I ain't never gonna git to play a game now.

[*He/she sticks his/her foot out, offering up his/her socks . . .*]

Sorry iffin my feet smell.

[*He/she spasms and shakes.*]

I hope the good lord don't hold my coveting against me and damn me ta hell, 'cause I bet they got tiddlywinks in heaven.

[*He/she keels over dead.*]

No More Sexy Vampires!

Carla Cackowski

CRAIG, 10

CRAIG *is dressed up as a vampire for Halloween. He is speaking to his younger brother Grant, also dressed as a vampire. But a slightly different kind of vampire.*

CRAIG   Grant! What are you wearing? No. Please. Don't leave the house dressed like that . . . We can't both be vampires . . . No, I said I was going to be a vampire for Halloween this year. Yes, I did. Yes, I did. Yes I did! . . . Just 'cause you're younger than me and Mom calls you her "baby" doesn't mean you get to do whatever you want. No, it doesn't. No, it doesn't. No it does not!

Okay, fine. We can both be vampires. Let's go. Just make sure you let me go first so that when people open their doors, they understand that you copied me and not the other way around. Grab your candy bucket. Where's your cape? . . . Grant, if you're gonna be a vampire, you have to wear a—

Ugh. I don't want to argue with you about this. If you're not gonna wear a cape, what kind of vampire are you? . . . Edward? Who's Edw—

No. No, no, no, no, no, no! Grant, you are not allowed to dress as the *Twilight* vampire! What's wrong with you? Edward is not a real vampire, he's a sexy vampire—and sexy vampires are stupid vampires, and stupid vampires are stupid!

Okay, Grant. Take a knee. Seriously. We gotta talk, bro. I know you're only seven and a half and that, at ten, I have the wisdom of time on my side, so I'm going to give you the benefit of the doubt here. Let me explain something to you . . .

Once upon a time, vampires were awesome. They were creepy and gross and people were terrified of them because they were killers. And then some girls came along and decided that vampires could be nice. They wrote these books and made these movies about vampires falling in love and holding hands and all other kinds of stupid stuff that nobody really cares about except people like Mom and her friends. It's true, Grant! It's true. And it's weird and it's ruining the vampire's rep. And we can have no part of it. Do you understand me?

Now, repeat after me: "I vant to suck your blood." . . . Sure, you can. Try.

Put the glitter down, Grant. I don't care if he's supposed to sparkle in the sunlight. Vampires don't sparkle!

As your older, wiser brother, I'm putting my foot down right now and telling you under no circumstance are you allowed to walk out that door dressed as Edward from *Twilight*.

Aw, come on, don't cry. *Sshh*. Don't cry. Mom will come if you cry.

Ugh. Fine. You can be Edward. Grab your candy bucket. Grab your [*Clears throat.*] glitter. Let's go.

Just make sure you stay behind me, okay? At least a few feet. I want to get a good scare out of the girls down the street before they realize who you're dressed as and ask to take their picture with you . . . I bet they will . . . I know, because the same thing happened to me two years ago when I dressed up as the werewolf from *Twilight*.

Over the Hill

Mark Alderson

JONATHAN, 8

Two young friends, JONATHAN *and Brian, are bundled up in the snow with sleds in tow.*

JONATHAN   Hey, I know this is a terrifying site, but just think about how fun it will be when we ride *down* the hill. Think about it, every kid in class has wanted to sled down Devil's Hump Hill but no one has actually done it. We can be the first! Imagine how Neil Armstrong felt when they told him he was going to be the first guy on the moon. He was probably pretty spooked, right? But after he made those brave first steps, he went down in history! Lets make history, Brian.

Now, I'm going to ask that you go ahead of me when we start walking up. It's not that I am afraid, it's uh, it's because I want to have your back. You know, I will be there behind you the whole way. So if you don't mind, I would like you to start walking up first.

[*Brian and* JONATHAN *start walking up Devil's Hump Hill.*]

Brian, do you think we can just like, go *halfway* down Devil's Hump Hill? No one is around except you and we can just tell people we did it. I will take a selfie as we go down and no one will know the wiser. [*Pause.*] Okay, you're giving me that look that I hate so I know you disagree with my plan, so let's move forward.

[*Brian and* JONATHAN *make it three-fourths of the way up Devil's Hump Hill.*]

This looks good, right? I mean, no one actually said where the top of the hill is. For all we know, *this* could be the top. I'm pretty sure I saw the top right around here in the springtime when all the snow was melted. Yeah, let's go down from here. [*Pause.*] All right, Brian, you're giving me the look again. We will move forward.

[*Brian and* JONATHAN *reach the top.*]

Phew, it's colder up here. Maybe we should head back down so we don't catch a cold. I don't want to miss pizza day at school on account of the fact that I couldn't keep myself warm. [*Pause.*] Geeze, Brian—Okay, I will do this. I know I was the one who talked you into this; I am just trying to stay happy and healthy.

[*Brian and* JONATHAN *sit on their sleds.*]

Okay, no turning back now. Brian, I want to thank you for encouraging me to do this. I'm pretty sure you're the Neil Armstrong in this situation and I am Buzz Aldrin. And even though Buzz has a cooler name, I think Neil was braver. Now, are you ready to make history for all third graders in Dutchess County, New York?

One small hill for mankind; one giant hill for eight-year-olds everywhere.

[*Brian and* JONATHAN *tighten their scarves.*]

Three, two, one . . . Blast Off!

[*Brian and* JONATHAN *rush down Devil's Hump Hill.*]

WEEEEEEEEE!!!!! This is amazing and I'm still terrified!!!!!! YAYAYAY!!!!!!!

[*They go down in history.*]

Packed Lunch

Cooper McHatton

SUSAN, 9

SUSAN *is eating lunch with her friend at school.*

SUSAN   My dad is really cool. Every day he makes me lunch for school. And his lunches are, like, totally AMAZING.

Every day he comes up with a theme and the lunch will look like that theme. Like space or dinosaurs or pirates and the whole lunch will look like a picture. Like a complete 3-D picture! For a pirate day he made a sandwich look like a pirate face and then he put all the other food on little swords and he wrapped cookies in gold foil to look like real gold! And then sometimes he'll do totally different things, like cutting words into cheese!

He'll also make little 3-D characters out of olives and hummus or rice and fruit or something. It's crazy.

Oh, and then there are his drawings! He does these really cool doodles on my napkin every day. Super-duper detailed drawings of all my favorite characters, and every day they're different. One day Princess Elsa, the next, SpongeBob. It's so cool.

And then he also writes these supersweet notes. Sometimes just "Good luck today, Susan" or something nice like that, but other times it's our favorite song lyrics or a poem. They are really sweet. Ever since Mom went to work and Dad's been home, he's really stepped it up. It's so nice that he takes the time to make these wonderful lunches for me.

[*Beat.*]

Oh, I NEVER bring them to school. No, I trade lunches with Tanner on the bus. He's really cool, and I think he likes me. He doesn't seem to mind taking the heat from the other kids making fun of his over-the-top lunches.

Return Package

Leah Mann

ALEX, 11 (gender neutral)

ALEX, *now a big sibling, stands in front of a nurse's station in the hospital.*

ALEX   Excuse me, nurse? Hi, down here . . . I'd like to make a return.

[*Holds out a baby bundled up in a blanket.*]

We got her last week, on Tuesday, and it was a big mistake. You can have her back. I don't have a receipt or anything, but I don't want any money back and I don't need a different one, we're fine without any baby. I don't know what my parents were thinking. They have me and I'm a handful. My mom and dad already work hard and their free time is full helping me with my homework and cleaning up and taking me to soccer, so there's no way they can take care of this baby.

And I am NOT sharing my room. It's a closet; there is no space for another person. This baby is defective anyways. I thought babies were supposed to sleep a lot, like that saying

"Slept like a baby?" I don't think that means what people think it means.

She's also NOT cute.

She's red and squishy. How can a baby look like an old man? It's weird.

Maybe there's a manager I can talk to? You don't seem like you know what to do. I know because my dad gets that look on his face all the time. Where's the baby section? I don't have all day for this. I have a huge project due tomorrow for history class. My mom is too tired from the baby screams to do anything and my dad had to go back to work already so no one can help me. It's lame. I have to write four whole pages about Benjamin Banneker and we aren't allowed to use the Internet or even spell check on the computer. No adults write stuff without spell check, so I don't get why we're supposed to spell everything correctly on our own.

I'm getting off topic. Unless you know a lot about Benjamin Banneker. Do you? . . . bummer.

So look, I know that babies are supposed to be good and I'm supposed to be excited to be a big brother[/*sister*], but I'm not. I never wanted a little sister[/*brother*] and I never will. I have lots of friends already who don't cry and don't smell bad. I don't like my parents being tired and grumpy. I REALLY don't like it when they yell at me just because I'm not being all lovey-dovey over her all day and then having to be ninja quiet so I don't wake her up when she finally does fall asleep. I'm not a ninja!

[*Beat.*]

Not yet, at least. I've been practicing and taking karate so it's only a matter of time, but it takes YEARS of practice to be a real ninja and it's not my fault if I make a little noise. I'm a kid! Kids make noise. It's a fact.

One kid is enough for any house and I existed first. I'm eleven for goodness' sake. I'm too old to be an older brother[/*sister*]. That stuff is fine when you're still a little kid and don't know what's going on, but I'm most of the way to being a grown-up—I can't have a baby dragging me back. Vacations where we have to do baby stuff? Movies for babies? Potty training and preschool and dumb baby books with cheesy pictures and single words like "cat" or "house." It's so BORING! It's not right to make a maturing person like me dumb down so a baby can feel included. Sure, I was into Blues Clues and Dora when I was little, but I grew out of it. I guess an older sister would be cool. She could drive me around and show me adult stuff and expand my horizons, but a baby sister? That's like de-expanding my horizons.

I'm just going to leave her on this table. She'll stop crying in an hour or so. There's probably some other family that doesn't already have a kid that'll want her.

Well, I should be getting home. Don't tell her new family how much she smells, or you'll never get rid of her. You guys should be more careful about who you hand these out to in the future.

Sitting in the Trouble Chair

Tiffany E. Babb

KIT/KIM, 10 (gender neutral)

KIT/KIM *is sitting in a chair directly outside of the principal's office. She/he speaks to the audience.*

KIT/KIM   If I were the principal, I would *never* make kids wait outside of the principal's office.

[*Beat.*]

Yeah, let's just put all the kids who get in trouble in this special trouble chair, so everyone who walks by knows that they got caught doing something.

[*Beat.*]

It's not like I did anything *really* bad. All I did was tell Dennis Carahan that he's an annoying poop face and everyone hates him. And it's the truth! Aren't you always supposed to tell the truth?

[*Mimics teacher's voice:*] *Not if it hurts someone's feelings.*

[*Beat.*]

Anyway, it's not like I actually hurt Dennis's feelings. He's *happy* that I got sent out. He even stuck his tongue out at me when I left the room!

[*Beat.*]

Dennis gets away with *everything*. I mean, the only reason I said he was annoying was 'cause he kept throwing paperclips at me! We aren't even supposed to have paperclips in our desks after that one time when I made that really long chain and Marcy Chou accidentally tripped over and broke her arm. Whoops.

[*Beat.*]

And if I tell on Dennis for throwing paperclips, the principal's gonna tell me that it's not good to be a tattletale.

[*Beat.*]

Now you tell me, why does that only happen when I'm the one who's tattling?

[*Beat.*]

Whatever. Maybe I'll catch a frog at lunch and sneak it in his desk.

Your Pretend Skills

Gina Nicewonger

AMELIA, 4 to 7

AMELIA *thinks of herself as an adult and addresses her aunt about the way she plays pretend.*

AMELIA Aunt Becky, please have a seat. I'd like to talk to you about your pretend skills. I know you're trying really hard, but I know a lot about princesses and I think you need a little guidance.

[*Becky responds.*]

I'm talking about when my Princess Sophine invited your Princess Estranga to her birthday party. I asked you what your gift was, and you said? . . . [AMELIA *waits until Becky answers.*]

Exactly. A new dress. Aunt Becky, that was your ACTUAL gift for *my* birthday . . . for me . . . Amelia. I think you can do better. Princess Estranga could have gotten Princess Sophine *anything*.

[*Becky responds.*]

Right, don't say what you got me in real life. But, also don't say something you could have gotten me. That's not pretend. Think big, Aunt Becky. Picture the tallest tiara anyone's ever seen or a flying unicorn that can become invisible!

[*Becky responds.* AMELIA *is very disappointed.*]

What would Princess Sophine do with a spaceship, Aunt Becky? Princesses don't travel in space. Are you even trying?

Okay, here's what we're going to do. We're both going to have some quiet time in our rooms—you can use my mom and dad's. While you're in there, I want you to think about your attitude. After lunch, we'll try again. I want you to be your best princess. And Aunt Becky, please take this seriously. I really don't want to have this talk again.

The Not-So-Nice List

Andra Whipple

JAIME, 7 to 12

JAIME *is at Santa's Village at the mall, talking to a mall Santa.*

JAIME   Ah, Santa, we meet again. We need to talk. Last year I was very specific with you—a magic set. And yet when I looked under the tree on Christmas morning, I saw a board game that was clearly intended to be educational. Now, I understand that you are old, and when people get old sometimes their brains turn to jelly. But I also know that you are not *that* much of a jelly brain, because Alex at school *did* get the magic set. So it must be that I am on the Naughty list? False! I had done zero naughty things that year. And believe me, I was tempted. When Joe Miller had a Kick Me sign taped on his back, you will remember—because you are all-seeing and all-knowing—that I did not kick him. It was tempting, sure, because I'm the kind of kid that follows directions. But I knew that this sign wasn't really telling the truth, so I didn't kick him. When my dad baked cookies, I never *once* ate one without asking first. When my sister brought home her new boyfriend, I did *not* tell him about that time that she farted so loud she threw up a little in her mouth. I was more than nice—I was fantastic. I was great. I was award-winningly not-naughty.

Although, I guess it is possible that it wasn't so nice of me to put the Kick Me sign on Joe Miller's back in the first place. But I was just trying to make sure that a few more kids got on the Naughty list, in case the obstacle between me and my toy was a lack of available resources. And besides, if the kids that *did* kick Joe Miller hadn't seen the Kick Me sign, they probably would have done something else naughty. They had naughtiness in their hearts, and I just helped you see it. I think that earns me something even better than a magic set. That deserves something really crazy, like a limited edition still-in-the-box Mighty Raptor Doll 2D.

I know what you're thinking, Santa. *Wow, this kid really did me a solid last year, and now I feel guilty about not getting him the magic set he really deserved.* Well, don't worry, Santa—I don't hold it against you. Accidents happen. Mistakes are made. The important part is that we fix our mistakes. Let me give you an example from my own life: Last month, I poured paint all over the carpet. And yes, I did it on purpose. Now I know what you're thinking: that *sounds* naughty. But here's how I see it. It was a mistake. Just like the mistake you made in not getting me the magic set. But just as I was so gracious and forgiving about your mistake, I expect that you will extend the same consideration to me, because you are a kind and generous man.

And in case you're wondering, I do recognize that I did *eventually* embarrass my sister in front of her new boyfriend, but we both know that was because I didn't want her to get stuck in an unfulfilling relationship with him and be unable to pursue her dreams. So again, something that you might have marked off in the Naughty column, I assure you should be in the Nice column. In fact, is there a Supernice column? A Super-Duper Nice column? Because telling my sister's loser boyfriend that I caught her doing kissing practice on his yearbook photo was actually very nice. I may have saved her life. We don't know that guy—we don't know what he's up to. He could have been a con artist. You know, the kind of person who lies for his own benefit in exchange for material gain? He might have fleeced us for all that we're worth! I not only saved my sister by sending him packing, I saved the whole gosh darn family!

You don't seem impressed, Santa. Look, maybe I am more Naughty list material. I mean, here I am, monopolizing your time, making other kids wait longer and longer in line while I tell you my tale of woe. But you know what would shut me right up? A magic set. Or a Mighty Raptor Doll 2D. Either one, I'm not picky. Just hand one over and I'll be outta your hair.

No, Santa, don't call my parents over. I'm sure they're really busy, and they did explicitly tell me I wasn't allowed to harass any Santas this year or I wouldn't get *any* presents. And I wasn't even harassing you, I was just kidding—all of that was a total joke. I am super happy with my educational board game. In fact, I think I'll just get out of your hair because that's the kind of kid I am—Nice list material.

Tooth Fairy

Alisha Gaddis

EMERSON, 5 to 8 (gender neutral)

EMERSON *has just accidentally swallowed his/her tooth and is petrified of what just happened and the possible effects.*

EMERSON   [*Screaming.*] MOOOOOOOOOM!!!!! MOOOOOOOM!!! Mom! Come here immediately. Please, Mom. This is a 9-1-1 emergency! I COULD BE DYING!!! MOOOOOOOOM!!!

[*Beat.*]

[*Near hysterics and talking a bit like he/she has marbles in her mouth:*] Mom. The most devastating, disgusting thing just happened! My wiggly tooth came out and I swallowed it! It is living in my body now! I have a tooth in my stomach! A sharp, horrible tooth! Mom! I could die! It could scrape the insides of me like a giant monster claw or grow tooth babies and march up my lungs and poke holes in my breathing tube or this one tooth can grow into a tooth forest!

[*Begins crying. Beat. Looks up hopefully.*]

You mean—I won't die? And the tooth won't have tooth play dates and live in me forever?

[*Beat.*]

You promise?

Okay. I believe you. But there is something even more serious, Mom. I needed that tooth to give to the tooth fairy. I was really counting on that five dollars going towards my Mega-Mondo Supreme Water Gun 3000 for the summer. I NEED to have a plan of attack against Ava. She is vicious with her water balloons. What am I going to do?!?!?!? Summer is coming!!!!

[*Beat.*]

You mean my tooth is going to come out in my poop and I can retrieve it then? Disgusting, Mom, and I am NOT that desperate.

The Package

Gina Nicewonger

MAX, 4 to 8 (gender neutral)

MAX (short for Maxwell or Maxine) is speaking to Miss Kimberly, his/her neighbor, about a package that was delivered to their doorstep.

MAX   Miss Kimberly, I'm so glad you're home! I've been watching your front door since the UPS man delivered that package this morning. Oooooooh, I'm just dying to know what's inside! I love a big box like this, cuz it could be anything! It could be books . . . or a clock . . . or a paint set. It could be just anything in the whole-wide world and that's sooo exciting! Miss Kimberly, I told my mom I was coming over to find out what's in the box. Do you mind if I watch you open it?

Oh, goodie! This is so exciting. I couldn't think about anything else all day. I asked my mom if I should put it inside our house, so it wouldn't get too hot or stolen. She said the UPS man knows where to leave it, but I wasn't sure about that. I don't think he cares what's in this box. He delivers so many boxes. I don't know how he can stand not knowing what's inside all of them! It's so exciting!

Be careful with those scissors, Miss Kimberly. If you got something really nice in there, you don't want to scratch it. [MAX *is extremely excited.*] Ahhhhh. This is the moment we've all been waiting for! You cut the tape. You cut the tape. Gosh, you're just ripping it open! Wait! This is so exciting; you need a drum roll or something!

[MAX *creates a drum roll by patting his/her legs rapidly.*]

Oh my gosh. Oh my gosh! You're smiling. It's something funny. I bet it's really cool. I can't stand it! I can't stand it! What inside????? Let me see! Let me seeeeee!

[MAX *speaks very slowly. He might be disappointed.*]

Wow. It's toilet paper.

[*This is actually the best thing* MAX *has EVER seen.*]

I. Have. That exact. Toilet paper. At my house!!!!!!!!!! Ahhhhhhhhhh! We have the same thiiiiiing! That's sooooo cooooool!!!!! [*Jumping up and down.*] I use toilet paper AND Miss Kimberly uses toilet paper AND, it's the same kind of toilet paper! Ahhhhhhhhhh! Oh my gosh! Oh my gosh! I can't believe it! This is amazing! [*Taking a big breath.*] Wow. I'm so glad I found out what was in that box! My mom said it probably wouldn't be that exacting. Boy, was she wrong!

Star Wars: The Discovery

Keisha Cosand

JACK, 8 to 10

JACK *is watching* Star Wars: The Return of the Jedi *for the first time, at home with his father.*

JACK   Dad, this is so awesome! *Star Wars* is the best movie ever! How come no one knows about it? Oh . . . they do? Oh . . . Anyway, R2-D2 is totally cool, and now I know why you sometimes call Mom C-3PO. He's nice but a real pansy and uptight like Mom. Don't tell her I said that!

No! I don't want to be Luke—he's kind of dumb. I know the force is with him and stuff, and Yoda is like, "Luke, when gone am I . . . the last of the Jedi will you be." And it's sad that Darth Vader is his father, but Han Solo is WAY more exciting. I'm glad Leia hooks up with him and not Luke, especially since Luke IS HER BROTHER! I'm still trying to figure out her hair, though. It's like she wrapped it around giant sticky buns.

Whoa! Slow down, Dad. When did Luke live in the desert, and when was Obi-Wan Kenobi alive? Are you telling me this is not the first movie? There is more than one?! *Return of the Jedi* isn't the first?! YOU LET ME WATCH THEM OUT OF ORDER?! TURN IT OFF! TURN IT OFF! [JACK *closes his eyes, covers his ears, and turns his head away from the screen.*] I have to see the other one first! [JACK *takes a few seconds to breathe deeply and collect himself.*] Okay [*He takes one more deep cleansing breath with eyes closed, raises his arms over his head then brings them down in prayer position in front of his chest, then opens his eyes.*] . . . just tell me one more thing: does Chewbacca eat an Ewok?

Throwing in the Space Towel

JP Karliak

JO, 6 to 10 (gender neutral)

JO is an adventurous kid. But every adventure has to end sometime.

JO   Mom, I have something to tell you. The past few months have been really rough. Nobody said this is easy, but after a lot of self-reflection, I've come to an important decision. There comes a time you have to think of yourself first. And I want to leave while I'm remembered for the good I've done, not the mistakes I've made. So, it's with a heavy heart I announce my retirement. No, dance class is fine. I'm retiring from being a Galaxy Ninja Spy Hero. I'm sure this might come as a surprise. I can't believe I'm saying it. But the recent injuries I've had make it impossible for me to continue.

I'm glad you asked which injuries. I'll show you:

[Points to elbow.]

This one from when Private Wesley and I were fighting the evil Emperor Buster on the Planet Backyardia. I had the emperor captured on his leash, but then he lunged after a squirrel and I tripped.

[*Points to knee.*]

This one is from when Captain Jermaine Lewis gave me a ride in his speed transport toward the Planetary Senate. He lost control and we crashed into the back of Mrs. Welby's Honda Civic.

[*Points to back of head.*]

You can't really see this one, since the surgical team on the Panda Bear space station is top-notch. But it's a gash from when I caught the traitor John Nable stealing vital rations of Gummi Worms from our secret orbital fortress. I tried to take them back from him, but he hit me in the back of the head with a space branch. Okay, it was just a branch. No, do not tell his mother, I don't care, and he's a traitor and I hate him!

Anyway.

[*Points to pinky finger.*]

This one is the straw that broke the space camel's back. Me and Doctor Surgeon General Mindy were climbing a rocket launch tower in the Desert of Sad Cat. We were chasing Chloe the Conqueror who was going to use her heat gun to destroy the rocket, ending life on every planet everywhere anytime. We had just about reached her when Mindy slipped! I reached out to save her from doom, and she only could grab my pinky finger. I saved her, but my pinky hurts now. And it's hard to wiggle. Which is one of the most important skills for being a Galaxy Ninja Spy Hero.

Anyway, I think the Earth will stay safe even after I retire. Chloe the Conqueror felt bad that I got hurt so she's a good guy now. And I told Doctor Mindy and Private Wesley that I'm always available for special assignment, and that my duties as Sea Turtle Rider for the Underwater Pirate Squad won't change. But I have to focus on my health right now. And take some time to reflect on my mistakes on the job. I hope you understand.

[*Points to forehead.*]

Oh, this? That's from dance class when John Nable and I spun around too much and fell. It was funny.

John Nable? Of course we're still friends, Mom—weren't you listening!? Anyway, this concludes my announcement. I'd like some ice cream now.

Hiding

Alessandra Rizzotti

CARINE, 12

CARINE *talks to her friend Ashley about diet while trying on clothes at a department store in a dressing room, and it's for a specific reason. She's been depriving herself of food on purpose and she doesn't know why, other than the fact she wishes she were skinnier. From the conversation, she realizes she has a bigger problem and needs help.*

CARINE Ashley, do you like this dress? Like do you think it makes me look fat?

[CARINE *looks at herself in the mirror and holds in her stomach then tries to suck her face in like a fish.*]

What about now? You sure? My mom keeps telling me I need a thigh gap and less pudge in my belly and so I can never tell if things look good on me anymore.

[CARINE *tries to suck in her gut.*]

You know how you're a vegetarian? You don't eat meat, right? What is that like? Do you hate that you don't eat meat or do you just hate meat? Or do you like vegetables enough to be okay with not eating meat? I can't imagine eating just vegetables, but then again, I can't really imagine eating lately. It's like I have no appetite. Everything tastes bad. It's like I'm not hungry, or something. But then, at night, late at night, when it gets to be midnight, I sneak into the kitchen and I eat a lot of cookie dough. My mom doesn't know. I know that's like not being vegetarian or anything, but maybe it's like being a cookierarian?

No, it's not a sugar addiction. Or maybe it is. I eat almost all the cookie dough and also any sugar that's there, like whip cream, ice cream, and chocolate-covered raisins (which are healthier, but still). And then, when I get really full, it's like I don't want any of the food anymore and I feel sick, so I have to throw it all up.

[CARINE *turns her head to the door, as if someone tried to open it.*]

Excuse me, we're in here! Jeez. People have no respect.

Anyways . . . it's really weird. And I don't want my mom to hear me, so I don't throw up in the bathroom. I throw up in my pillow and then I put it in a plastic bag and take it to school, and throw it away there. It's so gross, but I'm scared she will find out then get mad at me for eating all the cookie dough. Not that she hasn't noticed. She's also been wondering where all the pillowcases have gone, but I have this plan to tell her that it's the maid. The maid just really likes cookie dough and pillowcases. She'll believe me, I think.

[CARINE *holds up some shorts to Ashley.*]

Do you like these shorts? Too green, right? . . . I'm not sick right now. Just at night.

[CARINE *tries on a bra.*]

My bra size is getting smaller, which sucks . . . That's such a sexy pinstripe pin skirt, by the way. Totally get it. Isn't Forever 21 the best?

. . . What do you mean by "eating disorder"? Does that mean I'm crazy? I thought only models had those . . . I can't tell my mom, Ashley! She's like the queen of being skinny! She wants me skinny. She doesn't want me when I'm fat. I know I can be normal again. I think I can do it. Just don't tell anyone. I gotta figure this out on my own.

[CARINE *holds up two pairs of pants.*]

Which jeans do you like better, flare or boy cut? I can't decide.

Shit. I can't even figure out what jeans I like. I definitely can't figure this out on my own. I don't want my mom to fire the maid because of the pillowcases and cookie dough. I have to say something. I have to own up to doing it. I'll say that I used the pillowcases for an art project and that I steal the cookie dough for our after-school lunch program and that I . . . no I can't tell her! I can't!

[*Ashley tells* CARINE *to practice telling her mom with her.*]

Okay . . . let me pretend you're my mom, then. Mom . . . I think I have a problem.

[CARINE *breaks the moment as if she's talking to Ashley again.*]

Should I wear this business jacket so she takes me seriously?

[CARINE *puts on the jacket, pulls on the sides of it, stares at the mirror, and breathes in deeply.*]

You know how you said the cookie dough has been missing the last two months? I've been eating it. Late at night. Like a cookie dough monster. It's like *If You Give a Mouse a Cookie* . . . sorta . . . I don't really remember the book . . . Oh, and I've been barfing in all the pillowcases, so I'll have to get you some more Bed Bath & Beyond coupons since they never expire . . .

[*Someone knocks on the door.*]

We're not done yet! We plan on buying the whole store, so leave us alone! Ashley, how much cash do you have? I don't think I can really buy the whole store . . .

The Slumber Party Is Over

Alessandra Rizzotti

DANIEL, 8

DANIEL *talks to his younger sister, Nisha, age 6, about their parents getting a divorce, as he understands what divorce is.*

DANIEL Nisha, don't tell Mommy, but yesterday I heard Daddy say on the phone that he's getting a divorce. Do you know what that means? That means no more slumber parties at our house. Daddy and Mommy will have to have their own slumber parties outside of the house. Like Mommy will be in one house and Daddy will be in another house, having their separate slumber parties. Ugh. This sucks. How are we going to surprise them every morning now with our silly walks and silly dances if they're doing separate slumber parties?

I don't know what that means for us. Maybe you will have to go to Mommy's slumber party and I'll have to go to Daddy's slumber party? Seems complicated. I wouldn't want to not see you, but it seems like the most practical thing to do because eventually, you're going to get boobs and stuff and only Mommy will know how to deal with that.

Seems like divorce is dumb, though. Aren't two houses more expensive than one house? I know our playhouse was two hundred dollars because I saw it in the Toys"R"Us catalogue, so imagine five hundred playhouses doubled up to make two different real houses for separate slumber parties! That's a lot of money. Do you even know what an apartment is? We might have to live in those and I hear they are small!

Does this mean we have to change schools? Where would you go if you could go to another school? I would probably not go to school at all. I would just make Daddy be my teacher. I know he's a lawyer, but he'd have to fit it in his schedule. I know Mommy takes us to school and sits in our classes, but he'll have to step it up if he is going to have a separate slumber party house.

[DANIEL *starts to cry.*]

This is just really surprising because I thought Daddy and Mommy were in love. I mean, they always have slumber parties and then they like to have dinner together, even though Daddy always comes home late. Mommy makes him those molasses cookies all the time. He doesn't eat them, but I think he appreciates it. Does this mean they don't love us anymore? Why am I even asking you? You don't know about relationships or love yet. You can't even spell.

It seems like we should write a contract about who we want to live with when Mommy and Daddy split up.

[DANIEL *gets on the computer and starts typing.*]

Okay, so, I'll go first. Number one. If Mommy and Daddy never see each other again, I'll have to live with Nisha no matter what, so that might mean living in our playhouse. What do you think about that, Nisha? I know we don't have a toilet or kitchen, but maybe we can borrow Mom's? That means we'd live in Mom's backyard, which we don't even know will exist soon.

[DANIEL *sighs. He seems overwhelmed.*]

I need a nap. Daddy is a lawyer, so maybe he can write our contract. Oh no, don't cry, Nisha. I think I'm just confused and maybe he didn't say "divorce." Maybe he said "horse"? Maybe we're riding horses this weekend? I shouldn't have told you. I'm sorry. It's just, who else can I talk to about Mommy and Daddy? Not Mommy and Daddy. You understand.

[DANIEL *hears someone coming up the stairs. His mom opens the door to say that dinner is ready.*]

Oh hi, Mom. No, Nisha isn't crying because you're getting a divorce. I mean . . . what? I didn't say that. I mean, you're getting a horse, right?

[*There's an awkward pause in the room. Their mom sits down to explain the divorce.*]

Before you say anything, we just want to know, where will our playhouse go and who are we going to live with? Can you just clear that up first? Also, just so you know, Nisha and I want to stay together, so we're open to getting our own apartment, if that's what it takes. I know I'm eight, but I can start working as a kid actor or something.

[*Their mom shakes her head, and tells them not to worry.*]

Oh good, so you're not getting a divorce and we can still have slumber parties and I don't have to get an apartment for Nisha and I? I don't want to be an adult like Justin Bieber yet, so please tell me we're okay?

[*Their mom starts to cry.*]

Oh no, we're not okay. Don't cry, Mommy. It's not that I don't want to be an adult yet—it's just that I don't want to become messed up like Justin Bieber is. You understand that, right? Are you going to be okay? Should we eat dinner up here, in bed, while watching cartoons? That seems like a better idea than at the table where you're probably going to get the divorce. I mean, horse. Come here, Mom. Give me a hug. I love you. No matter what. Even if I don't get our playhouse out of this mess. Just promise me that I will get a full year's supply of blue Play-doh. That's all I ask. Deal?

Okay, now let's eat. And then we can eat your favorite Ben and Jerry's ice cream, Chunky Monkey. Sound good? Gee. Divorce is really weird.

Wanted: A Superhero Sister

Kayla Cagan

LIBBY, 12

LIBBY *is in the bathroom that connects to her bedroom. She is getting ready for her first day of middle school, and talking to her reflection in the bathroom mirror.*

LIBBY   Sometimes, I wish there was someone around to explain to me how sixth grade is going to go down. This would be the perfect time to have an older sister, a sister who maybe also doubled as a secret superhero. Like if Mom or Dad wanted to ground me for two weeks, she would swoop in and say something cool, like "You can't do that to Libby! She's just a victim of circumstance! The neighborhood kids forced her to keep riding her bike against her will! Look at this face! Would she break curfew on purpose?" And then I would make a really supersweet face at them, like this.

[LIBBY *makes an over-the-top innocent face in the mirror.*]

My superhero sister would play some really dramatic music, like something out of a scary movie, and wrap her arm in mine and then, like, fly me out of my room, down the stairs, and out of the house before Mom and Dad could even say, "What were we thinking? Of course we can't ground our perfect angel!"

In a perfect world, my secret superhero sister would help me with all the really important stuff: picking out outfits, fixing my French braid, homework, getting un-grounded, and moving to a brand-new city where I don't have any friends or know any students at my new school, James Madison Junior High! Eek!

How am I ever going to do this?

[LIBBY *puts on a headband, and tries to get it to sit just right on top of her head during this next paragraph. She can play with it and make it funny.*]

I would even learn to speak French, say, if my superhero sister spoke French! French Club could be cool, and then I would be introduced as my superhero sister's sister and we would practice French together and say "Oui! Oui!" all the time and then maybe in high school we could go see the Eiffel Tower, like our cousin Nick did when he was a senior. "Oui! Oui! We are Le Superhero Sisters! Au revoir!"

But I have to face James Madison by myself, without a sister and without a superhero. [LIBBY *touches her headband, now perfectly in place.*] I guess I'll have to save myself, this time. [*In an over-the-top but funny voice*, LIBBY *jumps into another pose.*] Super Libby to my rescue!

I Don't Have to Explain What Love Is

Alessandra Rizzotti

LIZZIE, 12

LIZZIE *explains the love of her two mothers to her friend Jackie, who seems to be distant from her lately. They are on the same soccer team, and they're kicking around a soccer ball on the practice field.*

LIZZIE   Hey Jackie, I like your scrunchie. Good idea with the puffy paint. Anyways, enough small talk. Do you have a second to talk real stuff? Let's do some dribbling. You go over there and I'll pass you the ball. Don't be scared, I'm just going to get real with you, which you need to learn how to do eventually anyways.

[LIZZIE *kicks the ball towards Jackie and tries to corner her at the end of the field.*]

So, I heard you talking about my moms, and I'm just confused, because I thought you were my friend. Can I ask why you think it's weird for me to have two moms? Or do I need to scientifically explain that no, one of my moms is not my genetic mom, but she's raising me, so she's my mom, and no, I don't know the dad because he was just a sperm. Are you even in sex ed yet? You'll learn that when you get there.

[LIZZIE *starts to kick the ball upwards like a hacky sack.*]

Jackie, I KNOW you're Christian. We go to the same church. That's probably why you think kissing is sex. But guess what—everyone has sex eventually and if we didn't, we wouldn't exist. And good news is, Jesus loves everyone, including gays, so accept that he is into everyone. I know the bumper stickers say "Jesus Loves You", but when they say "you," they mean everyone, not just YOU. Jackie, you gotta improve your footwork. Your legs look like spaghetti. Just my two cents, but what do I know?

And to address your cafeteria Q & A about lesbian vs. straight couples, my moms don't kiss more than your mom and dad just because they're lesbians, Jackie. People who are in love express love in different ways. Some do it with gifts like dumb teddy bears, some do it by holding hands, some do it by doing laundry for each other, some do it by not screaming at each other. I don't know if your parents kiss at all (I'm assuming they don't since you seem weird about it), but people who love each other do things like kissing (preferably in private). You act like they kiss in front of your face all the time like weird teenagers at a movie theater, and I've never seen them do that, so why are you making that up?

Being mean and talking behind people's backs is not cool, even if you're popular and have the best Demi Lovato binders. My moms deserve as much respect as your parents do, especially because my moms actually care about our school and do so much for us, whether it's at the PTA or in our classrooms, cutting construction paper, grading papers, or making soccer snacks. Which, by the way, watch out. If you continue to be mean like you have been, they might just give you poisoned crackers.

[LIZZIE *kicks the ball towards Jackie.*]

Kidding. Have a good night. Think about your words before you say them. You're not a puppet. You have the power to change.

[LIZZIE *notices that Jackie seems down now.*]

Oh come on, turn that frown upside down! You have a cool scrunchie AND it matches our uniforms. I can't even match my socks. May peace be with you and let's beat those Tigers this weekend, eh?

[LIZZIE *kicks the ball towards Jackie.*]

Wannna Be in My Movie?

Bri LeRose

ALEX, 8 (gender neutral)

[ALEX *is in his/her living room, talking to his/her family. He/she holds a notebook and a big stack of papers stapled together, like a movie script.*]

ALEX   I wrote a movie, and you can be in it if you want. I need somebody tall to play the bear, because he's the hero. This huge bear that can read people's minds and also fly. It's smart, because people wouldn't think bears can fly, but this one can, which surprises people. Jeffrey—that's the bear's name— Jeffrey will be out in the forest, and he can hear somebody camping in a tent, and the person can be thinking about crimes like, "I'm gonna steal that car," and then Jeffrey flies over to the car and protects it, because he's a bear. He's like, "RAAAHHHHHRRR I heard you thinking about stealing this car, now get out of here!!" And then if the person doesn't leave, Jeffrey picks him up and flies over a river and drops him in, but only if the person can swim, because Jeffrey's not really mean.

If you don't think you can be brave like that and you don't want to fly, you could maybe play the princess. She's the funny one. Everybody thinks she's just this princess, and all she does is sit around all day and drink tea, but actually she's a comedian. When her mom and dad go to bed, she jumps out the window and goes to do comedy shows all over the place. She goes out there in her tiara, like, "What's the deal with glass slippers? Wouldn't you shatter them with your foot and get a whole bunch of cuts?" And everybody in the audience is like, "HAHAHA! Whoa! I didn't know princesses could be funny!" They love it. She's awesome. Also, instead of regular human arms, she has robot arms. I forgot to mention that.

But if you're not really funny, that's okay. You can play the villain in my movie. That can be a girl or a boy, it doesn't matter. The important thing is that the villain doesn't look like a villain—he just looks like a normal kid. He goes to school and has glasses and a little brother and all these weird freckles, which we could probably draw on your face with markers. But the bad thing about him is that he doesn't care about anybody; he just does whatever he wants all the time. He seems nice at first, and you try to be his friend or see if he wants to trade snacks at lunch, but he's not nice. He laughs at you. He says that your backpack is ugly or that he saw you fart when you didn't, and how can you even see a fart anyway? He tells everyone you got a D on your reading project, and that you cried and threw it in the trash when you thought everyone was gone from the classroom. So yeah, he's pretty evil. He's a huge villain, because he makes you think you're safe but then he turns around and attacks you like a raptor or an extra-mean cat. I know he's kind of a crazy character, and he's not super realistic. But if you're gonna be in my movie, you're gonna have to use your imagination.

If you're not great at using your imagination, you should probably just stick to Jeffrey the Bear or the Princess of Comedy. Those two are pretty obvious, right? Auditions are tomorrow at noon, in the dining room. Come prepared and don't forget your headshots.

Pageant Girl

Alessandra Rizzotti

EMMA, 8

EMMA *is a pageant princess and child model. She's gotten used to a lot of attention. She talks to an interviewer on the red carpet of her most recent pageant.*

EMMA Hi, nice to meet you, darling. My name is Emma Sitaro. I'm Miss San Pedro. I've been doing this for seven years and I'm eight years old. Sometimes I feel like being a child model is like going to be my life forever, you know? Like doing these pageants is not normal, but it could be my life forever, so why not do it while I still got it, right? I'm cute and spunky, and I better show it off till it goes away, right?

[*She winks at the camera, then gets serious.*]

I do, of course, have the aspirations—is that a word? . . . okay, cool—just checking. Anyways, I do have the aspirations . . . What do you mean what TYPE of aspirations? I have them, that's all I need . . . Are you speaking Mexican or something? . . . Oh . . . you mean what do I want to be when I grow up? Probably Instagram famous. Or maybe be a fashion designer. Or an astronaut, if we're all going to eventually live on Mars. I have to say, though, I like wearing all these poufy dresses and being the superstar of the night, with all my princess pretty makeup and capowy vavoom vavoom hair. I wouldn't trade it for the world, darling. And if I couldn't look this way on Mars, then no—I wouldn't be an astronaut.

[*She turns her face toward the sky and rolls her eyes. Then turns back to the camera, as if she's annoyed he's asking more questions.*]

Tonight, my talent is doing backflips. I've been doing gymnastics all my life, since I was two years old and I am eight years old now, as I said (bordering on not being a child anymore for pageants . . . *shhh* . . . don't tell). But anyways, darling, I'm super flexible. Like I can do the splits, after a flip. And I'm an all-star cheerleader. Also, I can spell. So I'll be spelling hard words and stuff for the literature portion of the pageant night. INDUBITABLY (i.e., "That's for sure"), I-N-D-U-B-I-T-A-B-L-Y.

[*She starts smacking her lips, blowing a kiss, then smiling, as if she's practicing for her finale.*]

My signature? What do you mean by that? Like what does my handwriting look like? I don't know, because I use computers . . . Ohhh . . . like what is the thing I'm best at? Um . . . probably the splits. But I dunno, that's for the judges to decide, darling, since I am amazing at a lot of things, including opera. Sometimes they just can't make up their minds about what I'm amazing at and neither can I!

Next week, I go back to school, which is hard because not everyone there understands what it means to be a pageant girl. They think I'm stuck up, but I swear I'm not. I'm just better. Like, I have more knowledge of the real world, you know? I can't help that. There's this girl Chrissy in my class who thinks she's a model, but she doesn't have an agent and she hasn't been around the world like me, competing in pageants. She might LOOK like a model, but she doesn't have the business sense, you know, darling? I have the business sense. I know how to invest my money into a college savings account already. I mean, I'm EIGHT. Hello. Clearly I'll be the CEO of a Fortune Fashion 500 one day. How did I learn this stuff? Oh. My dad is a lawyer. My mom is a PR agent. My grandparents were billionaires. I have privilege. Don't you?

[*EMMA looks annoyed at the interviewer. She turns and yells behind the cameraman.*]

Mom, get over here! Is this guy seriously asking me these questions? It's like too much already. Come onnnn! Excuse me, darling, but I have way more important things to do. Let's call this a wrap!

[EMMA *hands her mom her bag.*]

Mother, will you be a doll and hold my life for me? Thanks. That's a Fendi bag, by the way. F-E-N-D-I. Remember, don't touch it without wearing your gloves, Mom! Don't touch the F-E-N-D-I without those gloves!

The Ghost

Andra Whipple

CASEY, 8 to 10 (gender neutral)

CASEY *is talking to his/her dad in the living room.*

CASEY   Dad, I don't want to freak you out but I am one hundred percent certain there is a ghost in my closet. I am fifty percent certain it means us no bodily harm. I am twenty five percent certain that it is a friendly ghost. I am zero percent certain that it can just be ignored. This is the kind of ghost that needs to be heard. So, I propose we have a séance. And I anticipate your first question is: How did I learn what a séance is? I can read, Dad, and the library is full of books. Also, I know back in your day kids didn't have google, but I do have google and you can learn a lot just by googling "What does the ghost want to tell me?" I think this ghost has some unfinished business on Earth, the kind that only we can help them with. Based upon what I am ninety percent certain I've heard it say, I've developed the following theories: Theory one: the ghost is a Civil War veteran who died without confessing his love to a beautiful woman. Theory two: it's me from the future, trying to warn myself about the ghosts.

Theory three: it's an elaborate prank by a raving gang of
ghosts.

Now you may wonder, what makes me so sure I've seen a
ghost? Fact: I heard clanking in the night. And I know it
wasn't you or Mom because I checked the baby monitor I put
in your room, and you were asleep. Plus, it wasn't a human
clanking, more like the clanking of the chains of thousands of
years of ghostliness. Also, sometimes, when I wake up, my
encyclopedias are unalphabetized, and we know I would never
leave anything unalphabetized, so it has to be something else.
A message! From a ghost!

Stop shaking your head—I am being deadly serious. That was
not a joke! Stop laughing. Okay, not deadly serious. Seriously
serious. This ghost needs my help, and I need your help
helping it.

Our first order of business is tools. There are a lot of things we
are going to need for this séance. Number one: a Ouija board.
I know that Ouija boards are sort of the commercialized
version of a séance, and I want to assure you I am not a séance
sellout. The Ouija board is simply a last resort in case the
ghost is-slash-was the kind of person who is a sellout. Number
two: a flashlight. Obvious. Number three: a bale of hay. Also
obvious. And don't tell me that we can't bring hay in the house
because Mom is allergic—this is serious! She can take a
Benadryl for a few days. Number four: we'll have to invite all
of my friends over, because discovering a ghost can take a lot
of man power. Number five: pizza, for snacks. Because séances

can be very tiring, and we need something to keep our energy
up, I also recommend we get all of the necessary ingredients
for hot fudge sundaes, because we're gonna need the sugar.
Next we're going to need a variety of animals, like a horse, a
sheep, a goat, y'know, soft stuff, like you'd find at a petting
zoo, because it will make the ghost feel comfortable. And lastly
we're going to need a bouncy house, because at the end of the
day, ghosts just wanna have fun.

Now before you ask, I know you're probably thinking, has
Casey just concocted this elaborate story to get a free party?
And to that I say that, yes, a party would be nice. And you
know who really deserves a party? A kid kind enough to help
out a lonely old ghost. So, no, Dad, I'm not asking for a
party . . . I'm asking for help helping a ghost. But if you think
that makes me a super-duper person, the kind of person who
definitely deserves a party, then I'm not saying no. It would be
rude not to allow you to honor me for my selfless deeds. Okay,
fine. I lied about the ghost. But for such a good lie, don't you
think a kid deserves a party? We can negotiate on the bouncy
house.

Showtime for Jesus

Alisha Gaddis

BETHANY, 6 to 10

BETHANY *is a born performer and producer. She sees the annual Thanksgiving prayer as her "production" and does not hesitate to let her younger cousins know what needs to happen to make this show a success.*

BETHANY   [*Cupping her hands to her mouth.*]
Okay everybody. This is my big, our big, yearly time to shine and do the Thanksgiving prayer!

Let's get into prayer formation!

Line up according to height.

LeeAnn, switch places with Angela. She may be older, but you really had a growth spurt since Easter. Glad to see those carrots worked out! [BETHANY *just made an Easter joke and is pleased with herself.*]

Okay, guys—as your older and more experienced cousin, I am going to lead this off. We are going to file in, give a look of Blue Steel, bow our heads, and do what needs to be done.

Like I learned on the set of the major TV shoot for the Pheiffer Oldsmobile commercial I did—you can never care enough, and don't stop until I say "Cut"!

It's almost go time—I want you to go out there and give our family cornucopias of compassion, turkeys of talent, and awesomeness of abundance!

Let's practice really quickly! Repeat after me, head's bowed:

Thanksgiving, Thanksgiving, Thanksgiving—we are thankful!

[BETHANY *mouths the repeating.*]

Gobble, gobble, gobble up the goodness of life.

[BETHANY *mouths the repeating.*]

Amen!

Okay, guys—let's go out there and make our families proud! And Bryan—do not open your eyes to peek this year! I want to be able to talk to you at Christmas!

You're Doing a Great Job

Gina Nicewonger

JUNO, 8 to 12 (gender neutral)

JUNO *is speaking to his/her mother about too much parental praise.*

JUNO [*Unbelieving.*] I did a great job? I'm an awesome soccer player? That was an amazing kick? Mom, I scored a goal for the other team!

You're still impressed?

I couldn't have made a goal for the other team if I wasn't so fast?!? Get ahold of yourself, Mom. Do you hear what you're saying? That was an *okay* game, and I'm an *okay* soccer player, maybe even a *bad* soccer player.

[*Mom is getting upset.*]

Mom, Mom! Don't get upset. It's okay. I don't need to be great at soccer. I don't even like it that much.

Actually, Mom, that's not true either. I'm *not* a natural piano player.

No, I'm *not* the leader in my Taekwondo club.

I'm not the best artist in my class, or mathematician, or speller—I don't think. Maybe—but who even cares? That's not the point. You give me too much praise, Mom. And [*Trying to say this without hurting Mom's feelings.*] praise loses its meaning when it's not true.

[*Mom is crying.*]

Mom, Mom, don't cry. It's okay. All moms go around telling their kids they're the best at everything, so of course they can't all be telling the truth.

Oh, you wanted to be the mom with a really talented child?

Cuz, that would mean you're the best mom?

This must be really tough for you to hear. Well, I've never had any other mom, so I can't honestly say that you're the best mom, but I can say you're a really good mom. And coming from me, that means a lot.

Do you at least make the best chocolate chip cookies? Whew, now I see why this is so hard. JP's dad makes really amazing cookies, but you're good at so many *other* things!

Timmy Fell Down the Well

Leah Mann

LITTLE TIMMY, 5 to 10

LITTLE TIMMY *stands at the bottom of a deep, dark, damp well.*

LITTLE TIMMY   Gosh, it's really dark down here and my butt's all wet. [*Shouts.*] Hello!!?! Benji?! Mom? . . . MOOMM!!!?? [*Sighs.*] Carolyn?

[*Beat.*]

Lassie?

[*Beat.*]

I didn't even know people still HAD wells and now I'm stuck in one? Dad would say "This is classic, Timmy." Man, I'm going to be in so much trouble and I'm going to miss lunch AND maybe dinner and Mom is making kebobs and I LOVE kebabs. Everything tastes better on a stick—it's science.

[*Beat.*]

I messed up big-time. Is this what Dad means when he talks about consequences? That when you do something stupid then something bad can happen? Does that mean it's my own fault I'm hurt? I hurt myself by being stupid?

[*Beat.*]

I think I did.

[*Beat.*]

Whoa. It IS my fault.

[*Thinking it out.*]

If I hadn't stolen Carolyn's scooter, she wouldn't have chased me. If she hadn't chased me, I wouldn't have been riding so fast and I would have remembered to put on my helmet. If I'd remembered to put on my helmet, I wouldn't have gotten blood in my eyes when I hit the curb and smashed into that tree.

[*Getting more and more worked up.*]

If I hadn't had blood in my eyes, I wouldn't have run right past the mean guard dog in Mr. Jackson's yard and into the woods. If I hadn't been in the woods and too scared of the dog to go back the regular way, I wouldn't have gotten lost back here and been so tired and thirsty. If I hadn't been so tired and thirsty, I definitely wouldn't have tried to use that stupid old bucket to get some water and leaned too far over trying to get it out and fallen in when the dumb old rope broke.

[*Nearly in tears.*]

And now I'm sitting in the bottom of a well with nothing but a bucket and a broken rope and IT'S ALL MY FAULT.

[*Beat.*]

This is heavy. I think I just blew my own mind.

[*Beat.*]

What if I'm stuck down here forever? Mom and Dad would look for me, but they have two other kids and I think Benji is the favorite, so they might not be that sad if they can't find me.

[*Beat.*]

Maybe living in a well won't be so bad. There's water, even if it is kind of slimy. I can eat bugs; they're good for you. I read it in a magazine—bugs have lots of protein, and it's better for the environment than eating cows and big animals.

[*Beat.*]

There's a worm! Awesome, there's tons to eat down here. I'm going to do it . . . hey there, little guy. What's your name? Aaron? I'm going to eat you now, and I'm sorry, but it's me or you and I'm smarter than you and bigger than you so I win— it's science.

[*Beat.*]

Aw bananas, I can't eat that cute little face. I bet you have a family and friends. If you don't, I could cut you in half and then you'd have a twin. If you had a twin he'd be your best friend and would miss you a lot if I ate you. Then the only choices would be to eat him too so you could be together in my stomach, or to not eat either of you.

[*Beat.*]

I wonder if my best friend misses me. I miss him already and I've only been down here—gosh, I don't know, ten minutes? Maybe longer. Maybe it's been days and I don't even know it because it's some time warp! What if it's like Rip Van Winkle, and when I do get out of here it's two hundred years in the future and everyone I know is dead and I have to be friends with, like, people's great-great-great-great-great-great grandkids, who I might not even like!?

[*Beat.*]

I bet after a few years down here I'd start to get all wrinkly and pale, like not even human anymore. I'd learn frog talk and hang out with spiders and stuff. I could dig the well even deeper and live underground!

[*Beat.*]

Oh my gosh! There could be mole people or talking mice. I could dig all the way to the sewers, move to the big city and ride an alligator!

[*Beat.*]

This is the best thing that ever happened to me!

[*Beat.*]

Mom? . . . MOM!!! IS THAT YOU?!?!

[*Beat.*]

I'm down here in the well! It's a long story . . . I'm fine . . .

[*Beat.*]

Help me? No, don't get the fire department—

[*Beat.*]

Because I'm staying! This is my new life. You can come visit if you want, and maybe bring me snacks and a hat.

[*Beat.*]

And a shovel! Oh! And a leash for when I capture an alligator in the sewer world.

[*Beat.*]

Also my blankie.

[*Beat.*]

Thanks, Mom!!!

Punishment Worse Than Death

Andy Goldenberg

HARLEY, 8 to 10 (gender neutral)

HARLEY *is shocked when his/her dad takes away the iPad, sending him/her to his/her room.*

HARLEY   No! Dad! Don't take away my iPad! What are you trying to do, kill me?!

You are officially the worst parent ever! Worse than Jimmy Hoffman's dad, and he abandoned Jimmy when he was six. Maybe that's what I'll do. I'll run away. Like Jimmy's dad. I'll pack my backpack as soon as you fall asleep tonight and take off and never come back. Huh? Would you like that?

I'll do it. I will! I'm not being overdramatic. In fact, I don't think I'm being quite dramatic enough, because you don't seem to be getting it. I'll run out the front door and start screaming for help. I'll say you're hurting me, which you technically are, because you're essentially depriving me of any kind of happiness that I might have. What?! A whole month?

You're denying me a productive life, Dad. I can't keep in touch with my friends. I can't keep up with my YouTube subscriptions! I'll lose all my computer skills and not be able to complete any of my homework.

But maybe that's what you want. Hmm? You want me to be as smart as a second grader so that when I fail my tests and flunk my classes and don't graduate, you can point and laugh and say, "Ha-ha-ha, sucker! I got you real good that one time that I asked you to do the dishes and you didn't." My teacher'll ask what happened and I'll say that, hey, it's perfectly normal, right? My dad didn't want me to learn math at school—he wanted to teach me a lesson himself, at home. And, I mean, come on! Let's be real, here. I did NOT do the dishes. There were several glasses in the sink that needed to be washed and I'll admit it, right now, I fully ignored them. I clearly don't deserve an education other than learning that the most important thing in life is to scrub and rinse a few dinner plates. That's why I want to be a dishwasher when I grow up, Mrs. Cannon. That's why I'm dropping out of school, and living on the streets, because I ALSO had a tendency to leave the lights on and the air-conditioning running and . . . it's very hard for me to say this . . . but I never once actually mopped the bathroom floor. I just took some paper towels and wiped. I'm a bad kid. The worst. And I deserve to be punished. Nay, tortured.

Of course, it isn't really fair that Alex actually causes more trouble than I do, fighting all the time, staying up late, stealing money . . . but he never gets yelled at, does he? Remember that mug we got on our trip to Florida? The one you loved that broke? Alex did that. Never got in trouble. Meanwhile, I lose my iPad? Where's the justice? Where's the equality? Where's your humanity . . . you MONSTER!?

I didn't mean that. I'm sorry. Please don't take away my phone. It's the only thing I have left. Besides my computer. And my laptop. And my smartwatch.

Contributors

ALISHA GADDIS is a Latin Grammy and Emmy Award–winning performer and actress, humorist, writer, and producer based in Los Angeles. She is a graduate of New York University's Tisch School of the Arts and the University of Sydney, Australia.

Alisha's first book, *Women's Comedic Monologues That Are Actually Funny*, was published by Hal Leonard/Applause Books in 2014. Subsequently, she signed on with Hal Leonard to release five more books in this series, which includes the book you are currently holding in your hands. Her columns have appeared in College Candy, Comediva, *GOOD* magazine, and Thought Catalog. Alisha is the founder and head writer of Say Something Funny . . . B*tch!—the nationally acclaimed all-female online magazine. The highly irreverent Messenger Card line that she cofounded and writes for is sold in boutiques nationally.

Alisha currently stars in the TV show she cocreated and executive-produced, *Lishy Lou and Lucky Too*, as part of the Emmy Award–winning children's series *The Friday Zone* on PBS/PBS KIDS.

Alongside her husband, Lucky Diaz, she is the cofounder and performer for Latin Grammy Award–winning Lucky Diaz and the Family Jam Band. Their children's music has topped the charts at Sirius XM and is *People* magazine's No. 1 album of the year—playing Los Angeles Festival of Books, Target Stage, the Smithsonian, the Getty Museum, Madison Square Park, Legoland, New York City's Symphony Space, and more. Their song "Falling" has been used in Coca-Cola's summer national ad campaign.

As a stand-up comic and improviser, Alisha has headlined the nation at the World Famous Comedy Store and the New York Comedy Club, and has been named one of the funniest upcoming female comics by *Entertainment Weekly*. As a performer, she has appeared on Broadway; has performed at the Sydney Opera House, Second City Hollywood, Improv Olympic West, Upright Citizens Brigade, and the Comedy Central Stage; and has toured with her acclaimed solo shows *Step-Parenting: The Last Four Letter Word* and *The Search for Something Grand*. She has also appeared on MTV, CBS, CNN, Univision, NBC, and A&E, and has voiced many national campaigns. Alisha is a proud SAG-AFTRA, NARAS, LARAS, and AEA member.

She loves her husband the most.

Find out more about Alisha at *alishagaddis.com*.

MARK ALDERSON was born and raised in Phoenix, AZ, and currently lives in upstate New York with his amazing wife, Jade, and Australian Shepherd, Westley. He has studied comedy at NCT Phoenix and iO West, and can be seen in and around town performing stand-up. Mark would also like to say hello to his family and friends and promises to call them all soon. Feel free to e-mail him at *AldersonjMark@gmail.com* or follow him on Twitter *@MarkJAlderson*.

TIFFANY E. BABB is a Los Angeles–based writer and book hoarder. She just received her Comparative Literature degree at the University of Southern California. Babb enjoys reading novels, poetry, and comics. Some of her favorite writers include John le Carré, W. H. Auden, Emily Dickinson, and Jorge Luis Borges. When she isn't reading or writing, Babb likes to attend comic book conventions, eat brunch, and think about impending doom (usually at separate times). You can find some of her comics at *tiffanyebabb.com*.

CARLA CACKOWSKI is an actor, writer, improviser, and director living in Los Angeles. Carla toured the world performing comedy (on a boat!) with comedy troupe The Second City. She currently teaches improvisation to adults and children and directs sketch and improv shows at the The Second City in Hollywood. Carla has written and performed five comedic solo shows that have toured across the country. She's a member of The Solo Collective, a theater company in residence at VS. Theater in Los Angeles. Carla was a writer on *Lishy Lou and Lucky Too*, an adorably hilarious children's show that aired on PBS KIDS. Her monologues have been published in previous incarnations of this series, including the *Women's, Men's, Teen Boys'*, and *Teen Girls' Comedic Monologues That Are Actually Funny* (Applause Books 2014 and 2015). Carla really loves her family and friends and hopes that even if she never procreates, two hundred years from now someone will think of her when they read her monologues in this book. Find her online at *carlacackowski.com*.

KAYLA CAGAN is a writer and dramaturg living in Los Angeles with her husband and their dog, Banjo. She is a member of The Dramatists Guild and LMDA. Smith and Kraus publish her plays *Blue in the Face*, *Halasana*, and *Shot Americans*. Her play *Roller Coaster* is published in *Many Mountains Moving Literary Journal*. Her monologue "Dog People" is featured in the anthology *One on One: Playing with a Purpose: Monologues for Kids Ages 7–15* (Applause Books, 2013). Her ten-minute play *Band Geeks* was published by Applause in 2014. Her monologues "Margo Maine Doesn't Live Here Anymore," "Cannonball," and "The Peanut Allergy," as well as her ten-minute play *Fight of Fright* will be published in Smith and Kraus anthologies in late 2015 to early 2016. Monologues "No Time for Cults" and "Cindy for Goth Club President" will be published in at the Applause anthology *Teen Girls' Comedic Monologues That Are Actually Funny* in the winter of 2016 (also edited by Alisha Gaddis). Kayla has also written two comic books. Tweet and talk theater, writing, ice cream, and dogs with her at *@KaylaCagan*.

KEISHA COSAND is a professor of composition, literature, and creative writing at Golden West College. She is a fiction writer, poet, and dramatist. Her most recent work appears in *Words, Pauses, Noises* and *Yay! L.A. Magazine*. She lives in Huntington Beach with her husband, two young daughters, and ginormous yellow lab, Numan.

JESSICA GLASSBERG is a comedy writer and stand-up comedian. For ten years, she was the head writer on *The Jerry Lewis MDA Telethon* and performed stand-up on the nationally syndicated show five times. She has also written for *Zeke and Luther* on Disney XD, "A Hollywood Christmas at The Grove" for *Extra*, and The Screen Actors Guild Awards (where her jokes were highlighted on E!'s *The Soup*, EntertainmentWeekly.com, and Hollywood.com). Additionally, Glassberg was a featured performer on *The History of the Joke with Lewis Black* on the History Channel. In addition to her monologue that appears in this compilation, Jessica's monologues have also been published in the books *Women's Comedic Monologues That Are Actually Funny*, *Men's Comedic Monologues That Are Actually Funny*, *Teen Boys' Comedic Monologues That Are Actually Funny*, and *Teen Girls' Comedic Monologues That Are Actually Funny*. Jessica is also a prolific digital writer, with her work featured on HelloGiggles.com, Reductress.com, HotMomsClub.com, Kveller.com, AbsrdCOMEDY.com, attn.com, and Torquemag.io. She has her own blog called The Journey of Jessica: Comic Adventures, Misadventures and Misteradventures (with Little Moo) at *https://jessicaglassberg.wordpress.com*. For upcoming shows, clips, and writing samples, check out *www.jessicaglassberg.com* and follow her on Twitter @ *JGlassberg*.

This will serve as **ANDY GOLDENBERG**'s autobiography, in case you have to do some kind of paper on him for class. You can gloss over where he was born (RI), where he grew up (FL), and where he got his not-so-necessary theater diploma (University of Miami). Skip to the part about how he's Internet famous, right? His Goldentusk YouTube Channel (*youtube.com/goldentusk*) has more than 52 million views, with Time Out New York film critic Keith Uhlich nicknaming him The Theme Song Sondheim. In fact, *The Superman Theme Song* may have been the very first YouTube video you ever watched. He was a cover boy of the Nice Jewish Guys Calendar, won a game show, published a children's book called *Peter, the Paranoid Pumpkin*, and . . . you know what? Just google me. Check out *Youtube.com/goldentusk* and follow me on Twitter *@goldentusk*.

RYANE NICOLE GRANADOS, a Los Angeles native, earned her MFA in creative writing from Antioch University, Los Angeles. She has also attended the Bread Loaf Writer's Conference in Sicily, Voices of Our Nation Arts Foundation (VONA), and the Squaw Valley Writer's Workshop. Her work has been featured in various publications including *Dirty Chai*, *Gravel*, *Role Reboot*, *For Harriet*, *The Manifest-Station*, *Mutha Magazine*, *Specter* magazine, and the *Atticus Review*. Additionally, she teaches English at Golden West College and has authored a student success manual entitled *Tips from an Unlikely Valedictorian*. Ryane is best described as a wife, writer, teacher, and mom who laughs loud and hard, sometimes in the most inappropriate of circumstances. As a result, she hopes her writing will inspire, challenge, amuse, and motivate thinking that cultivates positive change. More of her work can be found at *ryane-granados.squarespace.com* or on Twitter *@awriterslyfe*.

JOSH HYMAN is a New York City–based actor, comedian, and writer. He studied at the Atlantic Acting School, performs stand-up comedy and improv on stages all around the city, and has competed in numerous IFNY Monologue Slam competitions, winning the Battle of the Champions in 2011. He is also known for his commercial TV work, appearing in spots for Dunkin' Donuts, Time Warner Cable, AT&T, ESPN, Jimmy Dean, Lowe's, Verizon Fios, Bud Light, and more. Josh is also a current and original cast member of the Off-Broadway smash hit *Drunk Shakespeare*, and has appeared on CBS's *Blue Bloods* and Nick Jr.'s *Team Umizoomi*. Along with developing the TV pilot *Sport Smart* and the web series *Let's Shoot Dirty*, he also produces YouTube videos—most notably the "You Down With JPP" song-parody sensation that accompanied the New York Giants' 2012 Super Bowl run. For more, visit *www.MrJoshHyman.com*; YouTube: MrJoshHyman; Instagram/Twitter: *@MrJoshHyman*.

ARTHUR M. JOLLY writes for stage and screen, and was recognized by the Academy of Motion Picture Arts and Sciences with a Nicholl Fellowship in Screenwriting. Jolly has penned over fifty produced plays, with productions across the United States and in Canada, Europe, Asia, Africa, and South America. He has not had a production in either of the Arctics yet, but has hopes. Published plays include *A Gulag Mouse*, *Trash*, *Past Curfew*, *Long Joan Silver*, *The Christmas Princess*, *The Four Senses of Love*, *How Blue Is My Crocodile*, *Snakes in a Lunchbox*, *What the Well-Dressed Girl Is Wearing*, and the short play collections *Guilty Moments* and *Thin Lines*. He is a two-time Joining Sword and Pen winner and a finalist for the Woodward/Newman Drama Award. Jolly is a member of the WGA, the Alliance of Los Angeles Playwrights, and the Dramatists Guild. He is repped by the Brant Rose Agency. His monologue "In Hot Water" is included in the collection *Women's Comedic Monologues That Are Actually Funny*. More information about him can be found at *arthurjolly.com*.

JP KARLIAK is a voice-over artist, writer, solo performer, and snappy dresser who hails from the "Electric City," Scranton, PA. His voice has fallen out of the mouths of Marvel heroes and villains, a werewolf nemesis of the Skylanders, and the self-proclaimed supergenius Wile E. Coyote, among others. On screen, he planned a fancy party for Sarah Michelle Gellar and delivered singing telegrams to *The Real Husbands of Hollywood*. A graduate of the USC School of Theatre, iO West, and Second City Training Center, he has written numerous short films and plays produced in locales around the country. His full-length solo show, *Donna/Madonna*, has garnered awards at the United Solo, New York International Fringe, and San Francisco Fringe Festivals. He can always be found at fancy chocolate boutiques or on his website, *jpkarliak.com*.

BRI LeROSE is a Los Angeles–based writer and comedian. She used to be a St. Louis, MO, teacher/grad student, and before that she was a Boston undergrad/filmmaker. Before THAT she was a Wisconsin kid/consumer of cheese curds. You can find more of her writing at *www.brilerose.com*.

LEAH MANN grew up in Washington, DC, and graduated with a degree in theater from Brown University in 2003. Since moving to Los Angeles in 2004 she has written several screenplays, television specs, short stories, and one novel that no one will ever see. Her short story "Going Solo" was published alongside work by prominent authors such as Neil Gaiman and Ray Bradbury in the horror anthology *Psychos: Serial Killers, Depraved Madmen and the Criminally Insane*. She is delighted to have a number of monologues included in the *Comedic Monologues That Are Actually Funny* collections for *Men, Teen Boys, Teen Girls,* and *Kids.* Leah currently works as a production designer, property master, and set decorator. She digs crosswords, her garden (get it . . . digs her garden . . .), and reads a lot of books. The dog she got after the *Teen Boys* collection was published is cuter than your dog. Find out more about her at *leahmmann.wix.com.*

MIKE McALEER is an award-winning digital cinema storyteller originally from Philadelphia. He holds an MFA in digital cinema and a BA in psychology, and has training in method acting and improvisational comedy from the Lee Strasberg Theatre & Film Institute, West Hollywood, and the Upright Citizens Brigade Theatre, Los Angeles, respectively. Mike firmly believes in the transformational power of cinema, and in his writing he aims to highlight relatable themes and struggles. In 2012 he founded Physiognomic Films in Los Angeles. Follow Mike on Twitter and Instagram *@mistermcaleer.*

COOPER McHATTON is a self-proclaimed tech and pop-culture geek. He cocreated Playfic, a website for writing and playing interactive fiction, which has been used as a teaching tool at numerous high schools and colleges around the country. He occasionally performs as a professional puppeteer operating big furry monsters in a family rock music spectacular. Cooper contributes frequently to family and pop culture blogs, magazines, and websites. He is known to be a fine curator of amazing things with small, devoted followings. Having never spent a day in a traditional school setting until he entered college at age sixteen, he never had the pleasure of experiencing wedgies or swirlies or any other similar types of torment and is pleasantly delusional. He's currently a math and comedy nerd and is convinced the two are completely intertwined. Cooper is your typical, ordinary, everyday, joyful overachiever. He's a vegetarian, an activist, a pacifist, and a ghost pepper connoisseur. He resides in sunny Southern California, which might explain his constant, overly happy disposition. Find out more about him at *cooperdiem.com*.

MARISOL MEDINA is a writer and comedian living in Los Angeles. She studied improv and sketch comedy at Ground-lings and Upright Citizens Brigade and has a BA in drama from the University of Washington. She has performed at The Comedy Store, Comedy Central Stage, LA Comedy Festival, and SF Sketchfest. More information about her can be found at *marisolmedina.com*.

GINA NICEWONGER has been "writing in the moment" by performing improv comedy for over ten years. She has written and performed in shows at the Upright Citizen's Brigade and iO West in Los Angeles, and The Annoyance Theater and iO Chicago in Chicago. She also wrote one-act plays produced by Studio C Artists in L.A. Other monologues by Gina can be found in in the men's, teen boys', and teen girls' editions of the *Comedic Monologues That Are Actually Funny* series. When not making stuff up, Gina enjoys teaching elementary school.

RACHEL A. PAULSON is a writer from Tampa, FL. Meaning, she grew up both on the beaches and in the country, the best of both worlds. After finishing school in Florida, she made the move out to Los Angeles. Rachel is a published online writer with the likes of SheWired, CherryGRRL, Your Teen Magazine, and iVillage. She most recently wrote the short films *Kleptos* and *The Chest* (which has just been accepted into the Cannes Short Film Corner. She is currently working on her first novel.

ALESSANDRA RIZZOTTI's pitch packets have helped writer Kirsten Smith (*Legally Blonde, 10 Things I Hate About You*) sell two films to Paramount and ABC Family. She's been published in three Harper Perennial books with her six-word memoirs, as well as three other monologue books for Hal Leonard/Applause in collaboration with Latin Grammy and Emmy Award–winner Alisha Gaddis. Alessandra has written for *GOOD*, *Little Darling*, *Idealist*, *Takepart*, *Heeb*, *Smith*, *Hello Giggles*, and *Reimagine* and has been featured on The White House blog for her work on the editorial series *Women Working to Do Good*. In her free time, Alessandra makes mixed-media art, one piece of which won an award from Leonard Nimoy and another that was featured in Miranda July and Harrell Fletcher's Learning to Love You More Gallery at the Baltic Contemporary Art Museum. Alessandra also beekeeps, edits children's books for 826LA (a nonprofit writing and tutoring center), and is working on a novel about finding her father. At *Backstage Magazine*, Alessandra strategized and wrote Twitter chats (in which she garnered seven million impressions) and edited casting notices, where she bridged the gap between filmmakers and actors. This year she was featured on PRX reading from her Mortified journal and wrote a poetry book called *Homegrown*. She is now the communications manager for the Trevor Project, a suicide prevention hotline for LGBT youth. More information about her can be found at *alessandrarizzotti.com*.

EMILY BRAUER ROGERS has written two full-length plays that were produced at Hunger Artists Theatre Company and two collaborations that were produced as part of the Hollywood Fringe Festival. Amazon Studios optioned her screenplay, *Romeo, Juliet and Rosaline*. Her work has been published in a Smith and Kraus anthology, *161 Monologues from Literature*. She has had short plays read and produced in San Diego, New York, Colorado, Missouri, North Dakota, Indiana, Los Angeles, and Orange County. Emily is currently a member of the Dramatists Guild and Fell Swoop Playwrights. She lives in Los Angeles with her husband and two kids, who provide comedy in her daily life. You can find out more at *emilybrauerrogers.com*.

KATE RUPPERT never really identified as a kid; she always saw herself as a thirty-five-year-old. She didn't do kid things and she didn't sit at the kids' table. Now she actually is thirty-five, and finally getting the chance to write monologues for rad and slightly unorthodox kids who are something like she was back in the day.

RIA SARDANA is a comedy writer and producer in Los Angeles. She blogs for the Huffington Post and produces for Mortified LA. You can find her in the cheese aisle at the local Trader Joe's or at the local dog park (she doesn't have a dog). Follow her on Twitter @*riahahahaha* or visit her website *riasardana.com*.

DANA WEDDLE is an actress, a comedian, and a cat lover originally from Norman, OK. She now lives in Los Angeles, City of Dreams! She has trained at The Second City Chicago, iO Chicago, iO West, UCB LA, and The Groundlings. Dana performs weekly doing live improv and sketch comedy at such awesome places as iO West, The Comedy Store, and UCB. She is really into hugs, winning grand prizes on game shows, and tirelessly campaigning for the addition of the breathtaking unicorn to the Apple emoji keyboard. Visit her website *danaweddle.com*.

ANDRA WHIPPLE is a writer, improviser, and comedy enthusiast who lives in Los Angeles with her imaginary pug, Winston. She has produced comedy festivals, written sketch shows, and even ridden a horse. She studies media representation of women and other underrepresented groups, and writes to celebrate all of the stories we haven't heard yet. She grew up in Centerville, OH, where she once played a purple crayon in a play. You can read the latest about her and her projects on the world wide web at *andrawhipple.com*, or tweet pictures of dogs at her *@whipsical*.

Acknowlegments

A lot of people are awesome. Some people are more awesome in regards to this book. They get extra thanks from Alisha Gaddis:

Thank you Sara Camilli—best literary agent ever. Without you, all of this wouldn't have happened.

Thank you, writers. You all put yourselves out there. It is hard to be funny, and extra super hard to be funny on paper in a particular format. You guys did it, and it is delightful!

Thank you Hal Leonard and Applause Acting Series (especially John Cerullo and Marybeth Keating). You guys have given me so much guidance, support, and freedom. I couldn't ask for more in a publisher and editor.

Thank you to Patty Hammond—copyeditor extraordinaire. You make all our funny ramblings readable and grammatically perfect. We ALL thank you for that!

Thank you, Mom and Dad. You put me through acting college, and never made me come up with a backup plan. That kind of support is the net to my freefalling ways!

Thank you, Ella. Your eleven-year-old POV really gave this book the perfect insight! Let's celebrate with frozen yogurt!

Thank you, Lucky Diaz. You are a pillar of hope and kindness. Thank you for being exactly who you are, because that is exactly the very best thing I could ever imagine. I love you, husband!

And finally, thank you to all the parents, grandparents, aunts, friends, acting coaches, and teachers buying this book for your little actors. By believing in their dreams and giving them the tools of the trade, you are providing them with wings to soar into the spotlight! I hope each kid thanks you during her or his Oscar speech!

Monologue and Scene Books

Best Contemporary Monologues for Kids Ages 7-15
edited by
Lawrence Harbison
9781495011771 .... $16.99

Best Contemporary Monologues for Men 18-35
edited by
Lawrence Harbison
9781480369610 .... $16.99

Best Contemporary Monologues for Women 18-35
edited by
Lawrence Harbison
9781480369627 .... $16.99

Best Monologues from The Best American Short Plays, Volume Three
edited by
William W. Demastes
9781480397408 .... $19.99

Best Monologues from The Best American Short Plays, Volume Two
edited by
William W. Demastes
9781480385481 .... $19.99

Best Monologues from The Best American Short Plays, Volume One
edited by
William W. Demastes
9781480331556 .... $19.99

The Best Scenes for Kids Ages 7-15
edited by
Lawrence Harbison
9781495011795 .... $16.99

Childsplay
A Collection of Scenes and Monologues for Children
edited by Kerry Muir
9780879101886 .... $16.99

Duo!: The Best Scenes for Mature Actors
edited by Stephen Fife
9781480360204 .... $19.99

Duo!: The Best Scenes for Two for the 21st Century
edited by Joyce E. Henry, Rebecca Dunn Jaroff, and Bob Shuman
9781557837028 .... $19.99

Duo!: Best Scenes for the 90's
edited by John Horvath, Lavonne Mueller, and Jack Temchin
9781557830302 .... $18.99

In Performance: Contemporary Monologues for Teens
by JV Mercanti
9781480396616 .... $16.99

In Performance: Contemporary Monologues for Men and Women Late Teens to Twenties
by JV Mercanti
9781480331570 .... $18.99

In Performance: Contemporary Monologues for Men and Women Late Twenties to Thirties
by JV Mercanti
9781480367470 .... $16.99

Men's Comedic Monologues That Are Actually Funny
edited by Alisha Gaddis
9781480396814 .... $14.99

One on One: The Best Men's Monologues for the 21st Century
edited by Joyce E. Henry, Rebecca Dunn Jaroff, and Bob Shuman
9781557837011 .... $18.99

One on One: The Best Women's Monologues for the 21st Century
edited by Joyce E. Henry, Rebecca Dunn Jaroff, and Bob Shuman
9781557837004 .... $18.99

One on One: The Best Men's Monologues for the Nineties
edited by Jack Temchin
9781557831514 .... $12.95

One on One: The Best Women's Monologues for the Nineties
edited by Jack Temchin
9781557831521 .... $11.95

One on One: Playing with a Purpose
Monologues for Kids Ages 7-15
edited by Stephen Fife and Bob Shuman with contribuing editors Eloise Rollins-Fife and Marit Shuman
9781557838414 .... $16.99

One on One: The Best Monologues for Mature Actors
edited by Stephen Fife
9781480360198 .... $19.99

Scenes and Monologues of Spiritual Experience from the Best Contemporary Plays
edited by Roger Ellis
9731480331563 .... $19.99

Scenes and Monologues from Steinberg/ATCA New Play Award Finalists, 2008-2012
edited by Bruce Burgun
9781476868783 .... $19.99

Soliloquy!
The Shakespeare Monologues
edited by Michael Earley and Philippa Keil
9780936839783
Men's Edition $12.99
9780936839790
Women's Edition $14.95

Teen Boys' Comedic Monologues That Are Actually Funny
edited by Alisha Gaddis
9781480396791 .... $14.99

Teens Girls' Comedic Monologues That Are Actually Funny
edited by Alisha Gaddis
9781480396807 .... $14.99

Women's Comedic Monologues That Are Actually Funny
edited by Alisha Gaddis
9781480360426 ...... $14.99

AN IMPRINT OF
HAL•LEONARD
www.halleonardbooks.com

Prices, contents, and availability subject to change without notice.

1015